Green Dragon Publishing
6 Liberty Square PMB#270
Boston, Massachusetts 02109

Joseph Warren
and the Boston Rebellion

Compiled & Edited by
Shane A. Newell

Green Dragon Publishing
6 Liberty Square PMB#270
Boston, Massachusetts 02109

Copyright 2017
Shane A. Newell
All Rights Reserved
Printed in the United States of America
Held by Library of Congress

Cover art: "Warren the Warrior" by historical artist Dan Nance, ©2017
Photography of Newell collection: Nicole Marie Newell ©2017
Layout design: Iconix.biz

First Edition
with 76 Signed & Numbered

Dedications

To my friends and fellow collectors Harold W. Reiser III,
Scott Mrosko and James T. Gennette

Acknowledgement

Diane, my wife and friend for more than thirty-five years, has once again supported my work. She is kindhearted and humble. She is as inspirational to me as any of my historical mentors.
Thank you Diane.

Contents

Dedications vi
Acknowledgement vi
Preface 1
Introduction 3
Part One
Enter Joseph Warren 7
Part Two
The Boston Massacre 13
Part Three
The Boston Tea Party 15
Part Four
The Siege at Boston 27
Part Five
The March upon Lexington and Concord 51
Part Six
The Battle on Bunkers Hill 71
Part Seven
Remembering Joseph Warren 93
Joseph Warren Bibliography 121

Preface

THIS BOOK IS A fine art memorial to Joseph Warren and is framed by previously published narrative accounts of the events that gave rise to the Boston rebellion. These works of art are from both early and modern times. Early portraits of Warren portray him as the genteel Boston physician. The paintings and engravings of Warren from the century following his death depict him as the Major General and martyr of the American Revolution. The modern paintings—some of which were commissioned for this book—are narrative portraits of Warren as statesman, revolutionary leader, and fighting patriot.

The Boston Rebellion, led by Joseph Warren, began with the Boston Massacre in 1770 and ended at the Battle of Bunker Hill in 1775. At the time, Boston was the revolutionary hotbed of Colonial America: British armed forces had seized the city and Joseph Warren found himself at the epicenter of the political and armed resistance. The historic accounts in this book are taken from original authorities, eyewitness accounts, newspapers, and letters from the time period. For a historic reading experience, the pages are formatted in colonial font and columns. Much of the narrative is reprinted from Edward Everett Hale's 1875 centennial publication, *One Hundred Years Ago: How the War Began*. Edward was the grand-nephew of Nathan Hale, a revolutionary war hero who was executed by the British in 1776 for espionage. Edward was also the nephew of Edward Everett, the statesman who was the master orator at the unveiling of the marble statue of Joseph Warren at the Bunker Hill Monument. To commemorate the event, The Bunker Hill Monument Association published a book entitled *Inauguration of the Statue of General Warren on Bunker Hill, June 17, 1857*. The book contains letters written by American dignitaries that pay tribute to the life of Joseph Warren and honor the sacrifices he made. Excerpts from these letters are reprinted in Part VII: "Remembering Joseph Warren."

Engraving: View of the attack on Bunker's Hill,
with the Burning of Charles Town, June 17, 1775
Engraver: John Lodge, British, active 1774 - 1796. Yale University Art Gallery.
Mabel Brady Garvan Collection 1946.9.104.2

INTRODUCTION

Having resided in two different towns and counties named after General Joseph Warren, I learned that during the one hundred years following his death, Warren was honored and remembered across the nation as the martyr of the America Revolution. Surprisingly, Warren's legacy became largely forgotten after the nation's centennial. Many modern history books mention him only as the fighting physician who was killed at the Battle of Bunker Hill. Sadly, his death on the battlefield had eclipsed the memory of what was in fact an extraordinary life.

There is a popular American history textbook[1], a thousand-pages thick, which introduces secondary school students to American history and the patriots of American liberty. Joseph Warren's name does not appear anywhere in the book. Given that several authors were involved in the work and that it was published only twenty miles from Bunker Hill, I am perplexed by their omission of a political and military leader whose name was given to 12 counties, 131 locations, and 5 naval ships.[2] This honorable recognition is certainly significant: During the reign of King George II, Joseph Warren was among the first to assert American Independence by writing a list of resolves in defiance of British rule. The Suffolk Resolves drafted by Joseph Warren were well-crafted and the only resolves to be formally endorsed by the Continental Congress. In a speech to the citizens of Boston, Warren foretold of the sacrifices necessary to decide the "happiness and liberty of millions yet unborn." These are words from a man worth remembering.

I find biographical and artistic interpretations from Colonial America inspiring, especially those made with some reverence for their subject. It was when I first set my eyes on the marble statue of Joseph Warren in the rotunda of the Bunker Hill Monument that I decided to create a memorial book. By publishing this book, I hope to reacquaint contemporary Americans with Joseph Warren and his role in securing American liberty. I hope you are moved as I am by the works of art featured in this book. If you are inspired to learn more, I invite you to consider the books listed in the Warren Bibliography and to explore the "high-minded patriotism and self-denying virtues of our forefathers." [3]

Shane A. Newell

---

1 BOORSTIN, D. J., KELLEY, B. M., & BOORSTIN, R. F. (2002). A History of the United States. Needham, Mass, Prentice Hall. Note: Needham is less than 20 miles from Bunker Hill.

2 FORMAN, SAMUEL, DR., Dr. Joseph Warren, The Boston Tea Party, Bunker Hill and the Birth of American Liberty." Gretna, Pelican Publishing Company, 2012. Print.

3 "Lafayette" The North America Review, January 1825, Print, page 179.

We want him in the Senate; we want him in his profession; we want him in the field. We mourn for the citizen, the senator, the physician, and the warrior."
Abigail Adams, July 5, 1775

N. Currier (Firm). (1840). Boston, Massachusetts. House in Roxbury in which Gen. Joseph Warren was born. As it was in 1840 [Print]. Retrieved from http://ark.digitalcommonwealth.org/ark:/50959/js956q37s

PART ONE
ENTER JOSEPH WARREN

ROXBURY, JUNE 11, 1741.

Born Joseph Warren, first son to Joseph and Mary Stevens Warren, growers of apples and British subjects under the Reign of King George II.

ROXBURY, 1755

"Mr. Joseph Warren [Sr.], of this Town was gathering Apples from a Tree, standing upon a Ladder, at considerable Distance from the Ground, he fell from thence, broke his Neck, and expired in a few Moments: He was esteemed a Man of good Understanding, industrious, upright, honest and faithful, a serious exemplary Christian; a useful Member of Society; He was generally respected amongst us, and his Death is universally lamented."
Boston Gazette, October 27, 1755

BOSTON, 1759

Joseph Warren, son of the late Joseph Warren of Roxbury, and former student of Roxbury Latin School has entered as a freshman at Harvard College.

BOSTON, 1762

Joseph Warren, recent Harvard graduate, has entered an apprenticeship under the highly esteemed Dr. James Lloyd.

ROXBURY, 1763

Dr. Joseph Warren begins treating patients. Warren is instrumental in the treatment of small pox in the Massachusetts Colony. His reputation grows due to his useful medical service to all classes of people. Warren publicizes his political objections to tyrannical rule and taxation without representation.

ROXBURY, 1764

Joseph Warren and Elizabeth Hooton wed. Warren makes ties with James Otis, Samuel Adams, Paul Revere, John Adams and John Hancock.

Enter Joseph Warren

(Left) Oil on canvas reproduction of the Peale-Polk original (above).
Catalog Number INDE14169 Independence National Historical Park, Philadelphia, Pa.
Attributed to a member of the Peale family, possibly the nephew of painter Charles Peale, Charles Peale Polk. It is thought to be painted after an engraving of John Singleton Copley's full-length portrait of the sitter.[1] Here, Warren is wearing a customary wig as he always had done. However, Warren's face appears younger in the "Peale-Polk" painting than in the two portraits painted by Copley. Unlike Copley's "full-body" portrait (the only known portrait from his lifetime), the Polk painting depicts Warren in some type of uniform—although the uniform does not appear to be authentically military or militia. Before Warren's death in 1775, the Continental Army uniform had not been invented. Many post-mortem paintings and engravings (including a later painting by Copley) depict Warren in an "honorary" uniform according to his rank as Major General. The Peale-Polk portrait may represent Warren as a Harvard graduate. While no depiction of eighteenth-century graduate uniform is known to exist, academic dress at Harvard had been described as a somber Puritan black being "relieved only by occasional gold-laced hats and coats, and a sprinkling of His Majesty's uniform."[2]

1. History of the Portrait Collection Independence National Historic Park Doris Devine Fanelli and Karie Diethorn, American Philosophical Society, Independence Square, Philadelphia, 2001 print.
2. Morison, quoted in Cynthia W. Rossano, 'Reading the Regalia: A Guide to Deciphering the Academic Dress Code', Harvard Magazine, May 1999.

10 Enter Joseph Warren

Photograph ©2017 Museum of Fine Arts, Boston
John Singleton Copley, American, 1738 – 1815
Joseph Warren, about 1765
Oil on canvas
127 x 100.96 cm (50 x 39 ¾ in.)
Museum of Fine Arts, Boston
Gift of Buckminster Brown, M.D. through Carolyn M. Matthews., M.D., Trustee, 95.1366

Enter Joseph Warren   11

The background elements of the painting—the column, landscape view, pink drapery and table covering, and matching pink chair—are Copley's creations, serving to provide a grand setting for Warren's likeness and to signal the physician's elevated taste. The chair, upholstered in a velvety material, has an exposed frame that is vaguely European in form. The sumptuous table covering is unlikely to have been used as such in colonial Boston, but instead reflects the convention in painting, popular since the Renaissance, of filling the background of portraits with luxurious fabrics. The white linen shirt, ruffled cuffs, and white silk stockings mark Warren as a man of some wealth and consequence.1 This representation matches the description of Warren as "a pretty, tall, Genteel, fair faced young gentleman." Handsome and charismatic, he was easily recognized in the flourishing city.

1. Description from the Museum of Fine Arts.

Detail: Dr. Warren's left hand resting on anatomical drawings.

12 Enter Joseph Warren

Boston Massacre Engraving by Paul Revere, caption: Paul Revere, "The Bloody Massacre in King-Street, March 5, 1770." Boston, 1770. (National Archives Identifier: 530966); Signal Corps Photographs of American Military Activity, 1754 - 1954, Records of the Office of the Chief Signal Officer, 1860 - 1982, Record Group 111, National Archives.

Part Two
The Boston Massacre

Account of Charles Hobby

Between the hours of nine and ten o'clock, being in my master's house, was alarmed with the cry of fire, I ran down as far as the town-house, and then heard that the soldiers and the inhabitants were fighting in the alley... I then left them and went to King Street. I then saw a party of soldiers loading their muskets about the Custom-house door, after which they all shouldered. I heard some of the inhabitants cry out, "heave no snow balls", others cried "they dare not fire." Captain Preston was then standing by the soldiers, when a snow ball struck a grenadier, who immediately fired, Captain Preston standing close by him. The Captain then spoke distinctly, "Fire, Fire!" I was then within four feet of Capt. Preston, and know him well. The soldiers fired as fast as they could one after another. I saw the mulatto [Crispus Attucks] fall, and Samuel Gray went to look at him, one of the soldiers, at a distance of about four or five yards, pointed his piece directly for the said Gray's head and fired. Mr. Gray, after struggling, turned himself right round upon his heel and fell dead."
signed Charles Hobby, a Boston labourer

***

Account of Captain Preston

The mob still increased and were outrageous, striking their clubs or bludgeons one against another, and calling out "Come on you rascals, you bloody backs, you lobster scoundrels, fire if you dare, God damn you, fire and be damned, we know you dare not", and much more such language was used. At this time I was between the soldiers and the mob, parleying with and endeavouring all in my power to persuade them to retire peaceably, but to no purpose. They [the civilians] advanced to the points of the bayonets, struck some of them and even the muzzles of the pieces, and seemed to be endeavouring to close with the soldiers. On which some well behaved persons asked me if the guns were charged. I replied yes. They then asked me if I intended to order the men to fire. I answered no, by no means, observing to them that I was advanced before the muzzles of the men's pieces, and must fall a sacrifice if they fired; that the soldiers were upon the half cock and charged bayonets, and my giving the word fire under those circumstances would prove me to be no officer. While I was thus speaking one of the soldiers, having received a severe blow with a stick, stepped a little to one side and instantly fired... On this a general attack was made on the men by a great number of heavy clubs and snowballs being thrown at them, by which all our lives were in imminent danger... some persons at the same time from behind calling out "Damn your bloods, why don't you fire". Instantly three or four of the soldiers fired... On my asking the soldiers why they fired without orders, they said they heard the word 'fire' and supposed it came from me. This might be the case as many of the mob called out fire, fire, but I assured the men that I gave no such order... that my words were "don't fire, stop your firing"... *signed Captain Thomas Preston, British Soldier*

Account of Danial Cornwall

Captain Preston was within two yards of me and before the men and nearest to the right and facing the Street. I was looking at him. Did not hear any order. He faced me. I think I should have heard him. I directly heard a voice say "Damn you, why do you fire? Don't fire". I thought it was the Captain's then. I now believe it" *signed Daniel Cornwall, a Boston Citizen*

Part Three
The Boston Tea Party

Original Accounts

THE DESTRUCTION OF TEA AT BOSTON HARBOR.

BOSTON GAZETTE,
December 20, 1773

On Tuesday last, the body of the people of this and all the adjacent towns, and others from the distance of twenty miles, assembled at the old south meeting-house, to inquire the reason of the delay in sending the ship Dartmouth, with the East-India Tea back to London; and having found that the owner had not taken the necessary steps for that purpose, they enjoin'd him at his peril to demand of the collector of the customs a clearance for the ship, and appointed a committee of ten to see it perform'd; after which they adjourn'd to the Thursday following ten o'clock. They then met and being inform'd by Mr. Rotch, that a clearance was refus'd him, they enjoye'd him immediately to enter a protest and apply to the governor for a pass port by the castle, and adjourn'd again till three o'clock for the same day. At which time they again met and after waiting till near sunset Mr. Rotch came in and inform'd them that he had accordingly enter'd his protest and waited on the governor for a pass, but his excellency told him he could not consistent with his duty grant it until his vessel was qualified. The people finding all their efforts to preserve the property of the East India company and return it safely to London, frustrated by the sea consignees, the collector of the customs and the governor of the province, DISSOLVED their meeting.--But, BEHOLD what followed! A number of brave & resolute men, determined to do all in their power to save their country from the ruin which their enemies had plotted, in less than four hours, emptied every chest of tea on board the three ships commanded by the captains Hall, Bruce, and Coffin, amounting to 342 chests, into the sea!! without the least damage done to the ships or any other property. The matters and owners are well pleas'd that their ships are thus clear'd; and the people are almost universally congratulating each other on this happy event.

Account of George Hewes

The tea destroyed was contained in three ships, laying near each other, at what was called at that time Griffin's wharf, and were surrounded by armed ships of war; the commanders of which had publicly declared, that if the rebels, as they were pleased to style the Bostonians, should not withdraw their opposition to the landing of the tea before a certain day, the 17th day of December, 1773, they should on that day force it on shore, under the cover of their cannon's month. On the day preceding the seventeenth, there was a meeting of the citizens of the county of Suffolk, convened at one of the churches in Boston, for the purpose of consulting on what measures might be considered expedient to prevent the landing of the tea, or secure the people from the collection of the duty. At that meeting a committee was appointed to wait on Governor Hutchinson, and request him to inform them whether he would take any measures to satisfy the people on the object of the meeting. To the first application of this committee, the governor told them he would give them a definite answer by five o'clock in the afternoon. At the hour appointed, the committee again repaired to the governor's house, and on inquiry found he had gone to his country seat at Milton, a distance of about six miles. When the committee returned and informed the meeting of the absence of the governor, there was a confused murmur among the members, and the meeting was immediately dissolved, many of them crying out, Let every man do his duty, and be true to his country; and there was a general huzza for Griffins wharf. It was now evening, and I immediately dressed myself in the costume of an Indian, equipped with a small hatchet, which I and my associates denominated the tomahawk, with which, and a club, after having painted my face and hands with coal dust in the shop of a blacksmith, I repaired to Griffins wharf, where the ships lay that contained the tea. When I first appeared in the street, after being thus disguised, I fell in with many who were dressed, equipped and painted as I was, and who fell in with me, and marched in order to the place of our destination. When we arrived at the wharf, there were three of our number who assumed an authority to direct our operations, to which we

The able Doctor or America Swallowing the Bitter Draught. Engraving London, 1774. Cartoon shows Lord North, with the "Boston Port Bill" extending from a pocket, forcing tea (the Intolerable Acts) down the throat of a partially draped Native female figure representing "America" whose arms are restrained by Lord Mansfield, while Lord Sandwich, a notorious womanizer, restrains her feet and peeks up her skirt. Britannia, standing behind "America", turns away and shields her face with her left hand.
Library of Congress Prints and Photographs Division Washington, D.C. 20540 USA http://hdl.loc.gov/loc.pnp/pp.print

readily submitted. They divided us into three parties, for the purpose of boarding the three ships which contained the tea at the same time. The name of him who commanded the division to which I was assigned, was Leonard Pitt. The names of the other commanders I never knew. We were immediately ordered by the respective commanders to board all the ships at the same time, which we promptly obeyed. The commander of the division to which I belonged, as soon as we were on board the ship, appointed me boatswain, and ordered me to go to the captain and demand of him the keys to the hatches and a dozen candles. I made the demand accordingly, and the captain promptly replied, and delivered the articles; but requested me at the same time to do no damage to the ship or rigging. We then were ordered by our commander to open the hatches, and take out all the chests of tea and throw them overboard, and we immediately proceeded to execute his orders; first cutting and splitting the chests with our tomahawks, so as thoroughly to expose them to the effects of the water. In about three hours from the time we went on board, we had thus broken and thrown overboard every tea chest to be found in the ship; while those in the other ships were disposing of the tea in the same way, at the same time. We were surrounded by British armed ships, but no attempt was made to resist us. We then quietly retired to our several places of residence, without having any conversation with each other, or taking any measures to discover who were our associates; nor do I recollect of our having had the knowledge of the name of a single individual concerned in that affair, except that of Leonard Pitt, the commander of my division, who I have mentioned. There appeared to be an understanding that each individual should volunteer his services, keep his own secret, and risk the consequences for himself. No disorder took place during that transaction, and it was observed at that time, that the stillest night ensued that Boston had enjoyed for many months.

During the time we were throwing the tea overboard, there were several attempts made by some of the citizens of Boston and its vicinity, to carry off small quantities of it for their family use. To effect that object, they would watch their opportunity to snatch up a handful from the deck, where it became plentifully scattered, and put it into their pockets. One Captain O'Conner, whom I well knew, came on board for that purpose, and when he supposed he was not noticed, filled his pockets, and also the lining of his coat. But I had detected him, and gave information to the captain of what he was doing. We were ordered to take him into custody, and just as he was stepping from the vessel, I seized him by the skirt of his coat, and in attempting to pull him back, I tore it off; but springing forward, by a rapid effort, he made his escape. He had however to run a gauntlet through the crowd upon the wharf; each one, as he passed, giving him a kick or a stroke.

The next day we nailed the skirt of his coat, which I had pulled off, to the whipping post in Charlestown, the place of his residence, with a label upon it, commemorative of the occasion, which had thus subjected the proprietor to the popular indignation.

Another attempt was made to save a little tea from the ruins of the cargo, by a tall aged man, who wore a large cocked hat and white wig, which was fashionable at that time. He had slightly slipped a little into his pocket, but being detected, they seized him, and taking his hat and wig from his head, threw them, together with the tea, of which they had emptied his pockets, into the water. In consideration of his advanced age, he was permitted to escape, with now and then a slight kick.

The next morning, after we had cleared the ships of the tea, it was discovered that very considerable quantities of it was floating upon the surface of the water; and to prevent the possibility of any of its being saved for use, a number of small boats were manned by sailors and citizens, who rowed them into those parts of the harbor wherever the tea was visible, and by beating it with oars and paddles, so thoroughly drenched it, as to render its entire destruction inevitable.[1]

1. George R. T. Hewes, A Retrospect of the Boston Tea-party, with a Memoir of George R.T. Hewes (New York: 1834), 37-41. Available through the Internet Archive

...I received your very kind letter, enclosing a bill of exchange of four hundred and twenty dollars, in favor of the distressed poor of Boston, upon Mr. Rotch, which I shall take the first opportunity of sending to him, not doubting but it will be duly honored. The sympathy which you discover to have, both in our sufferings and successes in opposing the enemies to the country, is a fresh proof of that benevolence and public spirit which I ever found in you. I rejoice that our friends in Philadelphia are united, and that all are at last brought to see the barbarous scheme of oppression which Administration has formed. ....
Any assistance, of what kind soever, that can be afforded us by our sister colony, in this all-important struggle for the Freedom of America, will be received with the warmest gratitude.
I am, dear sir, with much regard and esteem, your most humble servant,
Joseph Warren

The Boston Tea Party

In Photograph© 2017 Museum of Fine Arts, Boston
John Singleton Copley, American, 1738 – 1815
Mrs. Joseph Warren (Elizabeth Hooton) about 1772
Oil on canvas
127.63 x 101.6 cm (50 ¼ x 40 in.)
Museum of Fine Arts, Boston
Gift of Buckminster Brown, M.D. through Carolyn M. Matthews., M.D.,
Trustee, 95.1366

Boston, April 28, 1773

Elizabeth (Hooten) Warren has died. She is survived by her Husband, Dr. Joseph Warren and four children: Elizabeth, Joseph Jr., Mary, and Richard. Dr. Joseph Warren becomes a political activist, an orator, and Grand Master of St. Andrew's Lodge of Boston. He is elected President of the Provincial Congress and Chairman of the Committee of Safety. As Chairman, Warren is commander and chief of a civil defense counsel that is able to dispatch messages about British military activity.

The Boston Rebellion begins.

"Whereby the charter of the colony, that sacred barrier against the encroachments of tyranny, is mutilated and, in effect, annihilated; whereby a murderous law is framed to shelter villains from the hands of justice; whereby the unalienable and inestimable inheritance, which we derived from nature, the constitution of Britain, and the privileges warranted to us in the charter of the province, is totally wrecked, annulled, and vacated."

Joseph Warren   The Suffolk Resolves 1774

"Free America" was written by Dr. Joseph Warren, in 1774, and published in colonial newspapers. The poem was set to "The British Grenadiers," a traditional British tune. Note: Bostonians pronounced "America" with a long "a" sound at the end, allowing it to rhyme with "way" and "prey.":

That seat of science Athens,
And earth's proud mistress, Rome,
Where now are all their glories
We scarce can find a tomb.

Then guard your rights, Americans,
Nor stoop to lawless sway,
Oppose, oppose, oppose, oppose
For North America.

Proud Albion bow'd to Cæsar,
And numerous lords before,
To Picts, to Danes, to Normans,
And many masters more;

But we can boast Americans
Have never fall'n a prey,

Huzza, huzza, huzza, huzza
For Free America.

We led fair Freedom hither,
And lo, the desert smiled,
A paradise of pleasure
New opened in the wild;

Your harvest, bold Americans,
No power shall snatch away,
Preserve, preserve, preserve your rights
In Free America.

Torn from a world of tyrants
Beneath this western sky
We formed a new dominion,
A land of liberty;

The Boston Tea Party

The world shall own we're freemen here,
And such will ever be,
Huzza, huzza, huzza, huzza
For love and liberty.

God bless this maiden climate,
And through her vast domain
May hosts of heroes cluster
That scorn to wear a chain.

And blast the venal sycophants
Who dare our rights betray;
Assert yourselves, yourselves, yourselves
For brave America,

Lift up your hearts, my heroes,
And swear with proud disdain,
The wretch that would ensnare you
Shall spread his net in vain;

Should Europe empty all her force,
We'd meet them in array,
And shout huzza, huzza, huzza
For brave America.
The land where freedom reigns shall still
Be masters of the main,
In giving laws and freedom
To subject France and Spain;

And all the isles o'er ocean spread
Shall tremble and obey,
The prince who rules by Freedom's laws
In North America

The Boston Tea Party 25

Engraving circa 1775, morbidly modifying the Copley portrait of Warren.

"[Joseph Warren is]...the greatest incendiary in all America"
British Officer Lieutenant Lord Francis Rawdon.

Part Four
The Siege at Boston

Centennial Publication: *One Hundred Years Ago: How the War Began* by Edward Hale

In March [1775], General [Thomas] Gage, with thirty-five hundred men, was in Boston, looking for the opening of the spring, and hoping for re-enforcements from England. He had written to Lord Dartmouth, that, if England would begin with an army twenty thousand strong, she would save blood and treasure in the end. He had also sent Capt. Balfour, with a hundred men and three hundred stand of arms, to Marshfield, to encourage the loyalists there. The captain reported that they were well received; and the general felt encouraged to make new conquests.

He struck next at Salem, where he heard that there were some brass cannon and gun-carriages. Col. Leslie was sent out on Sunday, Feb. 26, 1775, to take them. He landed at Marblehead while the people were at meeting; but his object was suspected, and news immediately sent to Salem. When Col. Leslie reached the North Bridge, the drawbridge was up; and one of those parleys followed which, in all that history, showed how anxious were both parties to keep within the forms of law. The people who had assembled told Col. Leslie that it was a private way, and that he had no right to travel on it, or to use the drawbridge. He undertook to ferry over a party in two scows, known then and now, in the language of New England, by the proud name of "gondolas". Their owners jumped in, and began to scuttle them. In the scuffle which ensued, some were pricked with bayonets. The Salem people, to this hour, say that blood was drawn, and claim the honor of the first "bloodshed" of the Revolutionary War. This is certain, that they made the first resistance to a military force of England. Nay, there are those who hint, under their breath, that, after one hundred years, the Salem people would be willing to sacrifice a few grandfathers, if they could have the honor which, as things fell, has lighted on Lexington and Concord. It is no fault of theirs that they lost it. Leslie did not wish to force matters. Rev. Thomas Barnard, the minister, was on hand, as a minister should be on such occasions. He persuaded the colonel to be moderate, and promised that the bridge should be lowered, if the detachment did not march more than thirty or fifty rods on the other side. It was, for Leslie, a clear case of being "for the law, but again enforcing it." He agreed to this. The bridge was lowered. The guns had been removed in the meanwhile. The detachment marched its thirty rods, and marched back again; and Col. Leslie returned to Boston. A company of minute-men from Danvers arrived just as he was leaving town.

Trumbull in "Mac Fingal" gives this [poetic] account of this expedition: —

> "*Through Salem straight, without delay,*
> *The bold battalion took its way;*
> *Marched o'er a bridge, in open sight*
> *Of several Yankees armed for fight;*
> *Then, without loss of time or men,*
> *Veered round for Boston back again,*
> *And found so well their projects thrive,*
> *That every soul got home alive.*"

In the next number of "The Massachusetts Spy," the paper for March 2, 1775, one of the wits thus describes this expedition: —

"Caius Lessala was dispatched from Castellinum two hours after sunset, on the 5th of the Kalends of March (answering to our 25th of February), with near three hundred picked men in a galley, under verbal orders to land at Marmoreum, and proceed to Saleminum while the inhabitants of both places were engaged in celebrating a solemn institution. Lessala was not to open his written orders till he reached the causeway. He conducted the affair with a dispatch and propriety worthy of his character, expecting to find he had been sent to surprise one of Pompey's fortified magazines. But great indeed was his chagrin, when he read that his errand was only to rob a private enclosure in the North Fields of that village. He suddenly returned to Castellinum, mentioned some obstruction of a fly-bridge, and, not without a little resentment in his eyes, told Cæsar that 'the geese had flown.' " — Vit. Cms. Edit. Americ. Fol. 1775.1

Meanwhile Gen. Gage was feeling the country in other directions. As February closed, he sent Capt. Brown and an ensign, Bernicre, on foot to Worcester, to examine the country with reference to a march inland. That two officers of the army could not ride in uniform, with proper attendance, into the interior, was evidence enough that the mission Gen. Gage was employed in was hopeless. These two gentlemen went disguised as "countrymen "with " brown clothes, and red handkerchiefs round their necks." It is edifying to think of the skill with which two such Englishmen would maintain such a disguise. Bernicre's journal of the expedition is very funny. They travelled on foot, and were, of course, recognized every few miles.

Here is a specimen: —

"From that we went to Cambridge, a pretty town, with a college built of brick. The ground is entirely level on which the town stands. We next went to Watertown, and were not suspected. It is a pretty large town for America, but would be looked upon as a village in England. A little out of this town we went into a tavern, — a Mr. Brewer's, a Whig. We called for dinner, which was brought in by a black woman. At first she was very civil, but afterwards began to eye us very attentively. She then went out, and a little after returned, when we observed to her that it was a very fine country; upon which she answered, ' So it is ; and we have got brave fellows to defend it; and, if you go up any higher, you will find it so.' This disconcerted us a good deal; and we imagined she knew us from our papers, which we took out before her, as the general had told us to pass for surveyors. However, we resolved not to sleep there that night, as we had intended. Accordingly we paid our bill, which amounted to two pounds odd shillings; but it was old tenor. After we had left the house, we inquired of John, our servant, what she had said. He told us that she knew Capt. Brown very well; that she had seen him five years before at Boston, and knew him to be an officer, and that she was sure I was one also, and told John that he was a regular. He denied it; but she said she knew our errant was to take a plan of the country; that she had seen the river and road through Charlestown on the paper. She also advised him to tell us not to go any higher; for, if we did, we should meet with very bad usage."

They then took John into their company at inns and other places; and at Sudbury, at the Golden Ball, since immortalized by Mr. Longfellow, they were fortunate enough to find a Tory landlord in Mr. Jones. "Can you give us supper?" — "I can give you tea, if you like." This was the Shibboleth that revealed a friend of government [Loyalists]." Mr. Jones accredited them to other Tory innkeepers in the county above. They were sadly frightened on the rest of their journey; but till they came to Mr. Barnes's, at Marlborough, they had beds to sleep in. There their luck turned. No sooner were they under his roof, than Sons of Liberty began to intimate that they must not stay; and poor Mr. Barnes had to lead them out by a back-way. The tired officers took up their march.

"We resolved to push on at all hazards, but expected to be attacked on the causeway. However, we met nobody there, so began to think it was resolved to stop us in Sudbury, which town we entered when we passed the causeway. About a quarter of a mile in the town, we met three or four horsemen, from whom we expected a few shot. When we came nigh, they opened to the right and left, and quite crossed the road. However, they let us pass through them without taking any notice, their opening being only chance ; but our apprehensions made us interpret everything against us. At last we arrived at our friend Jones's again, very much fatigued, after walking thirty-two miles between two o'clock and half-after ten at night, through a road that every step we sunk up to the ankles, and it blowing and drifting snow all the way. Jones said he was glad to see us back, as he was sure we should meet with ill usage in that part of the country, as they had been watching for us some time; but said he found we were so deaf to his hints, that he did not like to say anything, for fear we should have taken it ill. We drank a bottle of mulled Madeira wine, which refreshed us very much, and went to bed, and slept as sound as men could do that were very much fatigued."

(cont'd page 47)

1. Newell: This anonymous editorial recasts the names of British officers in Greek and Latin forms. This classical style of writing was a popular form of mockery against British rule during the mid-eighteenth century. The Americans chose to portray themselves as the ancient republican heroes of the Mediterranean such as Cincinnatus, Cicero and Cato. There have been many artistic and scholarly comparisons made between the Rise of Free America and either the Rise and Fall of the Roman Empire or the Fall of the British Empire. For this reason, sculptures will occasionally represent George Washington and other American heroes in Ciceronian togas (one popular example is the Sir Francis Chantrey sculpture of Washington installed in Doric Hall of the Massachusetts State House in Boston). It is for this same reason that Joseph Warren notoriously wore a Ciceronian toga during his oration performance in March 1775. To learn more about this historical reflection, see the comprehensive work of Eran Shalev: *Rome Reborn on Western Shores: Historical Imagination and the Creation of the American Republic*, 2009.

Collection of Shane Newell

"Your fathers look from their celestial seats with smiling approbation on their sons, who boldly stand forth in the cause of virtue..."

Collage of Portraits: *The Sons of Liberty* by Artist Gregory Lawler

The "Sons of Liberty" by Gregory Lawler is a collage of portraits depicted in the manner of John Singleton Copley (1738-1815). Seated at the table are Boston's most notable revolutionary men, left to right: Dr. Joseph Warren, Paul Revere, John Adams, Sam Adams, and John Hancock. The allegorical scene of an evening meeting held at The Green Dragon Tavern was designed and staged by Shane Newell. Photograph Newell, 2017.

The Green Dragon Tavern was owned by the Masonic Lodge of St. Andrew where Joseph Warren served as Grand Master. Warren is dressed in black as was the tradition for prominent eighteenth-century physicians. Over his untied cravat, a silver Masonic insignia is worn to denote Warren's office as Most Worshipful. Although Warren is positioned far left, he is the focal figure of the painting. He is open, genteel, and sublime in his pose. His placement and black wardrobe represent his being the first statesman to die for the cause of American Liberty.

Adjacent to Warren, the virile tradesman Paul Revere is focused and brooding in his *hand-to-chin* pose. It is the same pose seen in Copley's painting of 1768. At the center of the table is John Adams, the Massachusetts' representative in the Continental Congress and future second President of the United States. Although John Adams was not known to be a member of the Sons of Liberty or the Freemasons, he attends the meeting and sits center stage holding a parchment document representing his many contributions to the formation of the Constitutional self-government. His body position is purposefully forceful and seemingly uncomfortable as a nod to John's admirable yet prickly personality. Wearing his powered courtly wig and cravat, he faces forward with his body turned toward his older cousin, Sam. The elder Sam Adams sits back in his chair appearing patient and calm, though he is a powerful instigator of the ensuing political rebellion. Sam was a prominent member of the Sons of Liberty, but he did not join the Lodge of St. Andrew. It is possible that his indifference for ritual and formality kept him from the Masonic ranks. On the far right, the wealthy merchant John Hancock is wearing a finely made blue wool frock with gold braid and buttons. Poised over his campaign chest, he holds a feather quill, ever-ready to boldly inscribe his great name. Detached from the moment, Hancock stares off scene with an aristocratic gaze. It is the same indifferent manner he showed when posing for his portrait by Copley in 1765.

On the table, a large map of Boston drapes over the foreground edge. Boston was visibly "on the edge" of war at the time: British forces occupied the city while Colonists held the surrounding farms and hillsides. The divide of loyalties between Tories and Patriots is represented by Benjamin Franklin's 1754 political cartoon "Join, or Die," which is only half-visible at the center of the table. Also half-visible on the side apron of the tavern table is the engraved "rising or setting" sun that foretells Benjamin Franklin's observation on July 4, 1776 about George Washington's chair at the Pennsylvania State House, now known as the Rising Sun Chair of Independence Hall. The busy scene suggests the momentum of this meeting: the men have gathered to address the predicament of the British Army occupation and how to battle the superior force. A small model cannon indicates the plan to commandeer and transport some sixty cannons from Fort Ticonderoga, a British-held post in northern New York. The plan proposed by John Brown and Joseph Warren, is to position cannons on opposite high grounds overlooking the city of Boston and force the British troops to retreat by sea. The plan was successfully launched when Benedict Arnold, Ethan Allen, and the Green Mountain Boys seized Fort Ticonderoga in May 1775. In December of that year, the young Henry Knox, together with a "train" of men, horses, and oxen began to transport the cannon some three hundred miles over lakes, rivers and mountains to reach Boston by February of 1776. General George Washington had arrived to execute the placement. That March, the entire British army and naval fleet retreated out to sea—the first victory for the Continental Army. Joseph Warren would not live to see the day.

Dr. Warren's Ciceronian Toga

Historical Interpretation: *Rome Reborn on Western Shores: Historical Imagination and the Creation of the American Republic* by Eran Shalev

Joseph Warren at the Old South Meeting House March 6, 1775.
Oil on canvas by Gregory Lawler
©2017 Collection of Shane Newell. Photograph ©Newell 2017

On the morning of March 6, 1775, Joseph Warren, a physician-turned-revolutionary leader, stopped his one-chair carriage in front of Boston's Old South Church. Warren climbed down from the carriage, followed by a servant holding a small bundle. The two men crossed the street and entered an apothecary's shop. When Warren came out of the store he wore a Roman toga. He now crossed the street once more and burst into the swarming Old South to deliver the fourth annual Boston Massacre oration.

Few events of the Revolutionary era offered a more stark reminder of the failures of the mother country than the Boston Massacre. In the course of that event on March 5, 1770, British soldiers shot and killed five Bostonians. The massacre was probably not the result of murderous intentions of the British sentries, as Americans claimed, nor an American plot, as some English did. The traditional patriot fear of standing armies, combined with the ominous ratio of four thousand armed redcoats to fifteen thousand Bostonians, led to the fateful clash, almost immediately named "massacre."

In March 1771, the year following the massacre, a committee on which Joseph Warren sat suggested an oration to commemorate the fateful event. James Lovell, a distinguished Bostonian, was chosen as the orator. Thus began a sequence of annual orations, remaining unbroken until its suspension after the Fourth of July celebration of 1783. These orations, according to Warren's contemporary, the physician and historian David Ramsay, were administered by "eloquent orators" in order to keep the revolutionary fire "burning with an incessant flame" for thirteen years (they were displaced by national Fourth of July celebrations after 1783). The orations were always published soon after their delivery and, according to John Adams, they were read "scarcely ever with dry eyes." Indeed there were "few men of consequence," as Adams further pointed out, "who did not commence their career by an oration at the 5th of March." The orators included illustrious names such as John Hancock, Samuel Adams, and Benjamin Church. Only Dr. Joseph Warren was chosen to deliver the speech twice, in 1772 and 1775.

***

Warren's political inclinations surfaced during the Stamp Act crisis of 1765. In a series of newspaper columns, he sharply attacked Massachusetts governor Francis Bernard and played an important role in the governor's resignation from office. After becoming a member of the Committee of Safety, a board of selectmen who dealt with security issues, Warren delivered the second annual massacre oration in March 1772. "The fervor" of the orator, remarked Warren's political foe and Bernard's eventual replacement as governor, Thomas Hutchinson, "could not fail in its effect on the minds of the great concourse of people present." The doctor was coming into his own as one of Revolutionary Boston's great orators. As the Boston Gazette reported, Warren's words were celebrated with "unanimous applause."

If there was one thing Revolutionary orators knew, it was that if you wanted to move people to action, you had to touch something deep within them.

Warren's reputation was built on much more than simply oratorical talent. He also had a gift for sharply worded revolutionary rhetoric, much like that of the still unknown Philadelphia pamphleteer, Tom Paine. In September of 1774, when the towns of Suffolk County met in convention, Warren delivered a paper, afterwards known as the Suffolk Resolves. These resolutions denounced the Coercive Acts, enacted by Parliament following the Boston Tea Party, as unconstitutional and therefore moot. They also called for the establishment of Massachusetts as a free state (until the repeal of the Coercive Acts) and the preparation of local militias for armed resistance. Warren's Resolves were forwarded to the Continental Congress, which readily adopted them. Early in 1775, the last year of his life, Warren became chairman of the committee of safety, charged with organizing the militia and collecting military stores. This physician was asked, metaphorically, to preside over an ailing body politic, providing it with the patriotic nourishment and the military arsenal needed for its restoration.

By March of 1775 unmistakable signs of a gathering storm were apparent. After the 1773 Boston Tea Party, in which 150 Bostonians threw 342 crates of tea from British vessels docked in Boston harbour, relations between Massachusetts and

"Dr. Joseph Warren," by renowned American Folk Artist Frank Finney. This portrait depicts Warren as he gives his dramatic oration at the Old South Meeting House in his Ciceronian toga on March 6, 1775. Wood and painted surface. Collection of Shane Newell. Photograph© Newell 2017

Britain deteriorated swiftly, until the colony was finally declared to be in a state of open rebellion. By early spring of 1775, war seemed inevitable. Warren thus staged his second massacre oration at a time when even the smallest spark would have inflamed revolutionary sentiments. And if the timing is any indication—the oration preceded the fateful battle of Lexington and Concord by a little more than a month—Warren's oration represented just such a spark. Nonetheless, it remains a largely forgotten moment in the story of the Revolution's early days. In part, this may be owing to the fate of the orator himself. Warren was killed by a British musket ball during the Battle of Bunker Hill several months after delivering his powerful words. Unlike Samuel Adams or Thomas Jefferson or any of the other familiar Revolutionary luminaries, Warren's role ended before independence was actually declared. And unlike so many other Revolutionaries, he did not survive to play a part in the creation of a new American nation. Whatever Warren's own fate, there is no doubt that the words he delivered in March of 1775 were a crucial ingredient in Boston's Revolutionary moment. There is also little doubt that they resonated for Bostonians for many years after the orator himself passed from the scene.

Revolutionary oratory was about much more than spoken words; it was also about a delicately formulated theatrical apparatus whose purpose was to transform mere speech into moving performance. For if there was one thing Revolutionary orators knew, it was that if you wanted to move people to action, you had to touch something deep within them. Taking their cues from the tradition of great Roman orators such as Cicero, they thus deployed a range of imagery designed to excite listeners' passions. Only in doing so, these orators came to believe, could the disagreement with Britain be transformed from a legal and constitutional matter to a matter for the passions—a matter of injustice, of dishonor, and of familial disgrace. As the reception of his oration suggests, Warren was a master of these techniques.

Unfortunately, it is difficult to know just what Warren's oratorical arsenal consisted of. Even though thousands attended the massacre oration, and we have several accounts of Warren's performance, reconstructing the event remains difficult. Nonetheless, there is much to be learned about Boston's mobilization for revolution from the events surrounding this singular act of public speaking.

"This day," the Boston Evening Post informed its readers on March 6, 1775, "an Oration will be delivered by Joseph Warren Esq., in commemoration of the bloody tragedy on the 5th of March 1770." But observant Bostonians recognized that this would not be just another commemorative address. The British forces now stationed in the city, Samuel Adams noted, were likely to resent any insinuation that their actions had been barbaric and would surely "take the occasion to beat up a Breeze." A later account reported that there was a "threat uttered by some of the British officers, that they would take the life of any man who should dare to speak of the massacre on that anniversary."

In his diary, Massachusetts royal governor Thomas Hutchinson recalled a larger assassination plot during Warren's oration. An English officer, according to Hutchinson, reported that if during the meeting Warren would say "anything against the King, etc., an officer was prepared, who stood near with an egg, to have thrown in his face; and that it was to have been a signal to

"Bust of Joseph Warren in Ciceronian toga." Medium and location unknown.

draw swords; and that they would have massacred Hancock, Adams, and hundreds more." The Virginia Gazette, reprinting a report in a London newspaper, elaborated on the awkward egg episode, claiming that "this scheme was rendered abortive in the most whimsical manner, for he who was deputed to throw the egg fell in going to church . . . and broke the egg." Tensions clearly ran high as March 6 approached.

The presence of a large crowd, including British soldiers, seems one of the few undisputed facts regarding the oration's unfolding. A nineteenth-century biographer of Warren recalled that "many people came to town from the country to take part in the commemoration," and Frederick MacKenzie, a British officer, reported at the time that an "immense concourse of people" assembled at the Old South building for the occasion. Both patriots and loyalists acknowledged the presence of redcoats in the crowd, and both confirmed the obvious point that for them this was a most offensive and most disrespectful occasion. Samuel Adams claimed to treat the "many . . . officers present" with civility as he showed them to their seats, so "that they might have no pretence to behave ill." The Boston Gazette, a radical patriot publication, labeled the "party of soldiers" at the Old South "perpetrators," claiming they came to harass the congregating Bostonians. Frederick MacKenzie claimed that "the troops conceived it was a great insult under the present circumstances, to deliver an oration on the occasion." Thus "a great number of officers," which Hutchinson estimated at three hundred, "assembled in the church and seemed determined to take notice of, and resent any expressions made use of by the Orator, reflecting on the Military." The hall was overcrowded, the audience filling the aisles, while the soldiers occupied the stairs, perhaps hoping to scare Warren into silence. Whether they were "many," a "party," or "a great number," as different accounts claimed, the presence of fuming British redcoats among the packed patriot crowd must have added an ominous sense to

But Warren would not be intimidated. In fact, if contemporary accounts are correct, his chosen attire—the plain white Roman toga—established a dramatic contrast between the speaker and his redcoat antagonists. It was almost as if Warren knew they would be there and chose the garment precisely to antagonize them. As they sat stiffly in their heavy red wool coats—the sartorial definition of Britishness—he would hold forth, in the flowing freedom of his billowing white garment—the sartorial definition of ancient, primordial virtue. Of course the garment's color was not its only distinctive quality. Indeed, one would be hard pressed to find clothing more unlike that of these British soldiers.

The toga was the principal garment of a freeborn Roman male citizen. It consisted of a single piece of material of irregular form—long, broad, and flowing, without sleeves or armholes, and covering the whole body with the exception of the right arm. Because it was worn without any kind of fastening device, the wearer had to keep his left arm crooked to support its voluminous drapery. What could be more unlike the stiff, tightly tailored coat, waistcoat, and breeches of the British soldier? In the toga, there was no artifice, no false front, no deviant concealment; what you saw was what you got. And the only thing that separated the wearer's body from his audience was that bent left arm. To wear such a garment, in other words, was to do

"General Warren was a Brother Mason — an active, zealous, honored member of our Order. He was admitted to membership in 1761, — when only about twenty-one years of age, — in St. Andrew's Lodge in Boston. Over this Lodge he was elected Master in 1769; and during that year so highly were his efforts to promote the efficiency and honor of our institution appreciated, he was promoted to the station of Provincial Grand Master. This office he filled to the time of his death, with great benefit to the Craft and honor to himself the punctuality and zeal with which he discharged its various and responsible duties are evinced by the fact that he presided at thirty-seven out of the forty communications of his Grand Lodge, held while he was Grand Master."

John T. Heard, Most Worshipful Grand Master of the Grand Lodge of Massachusetts, 1857

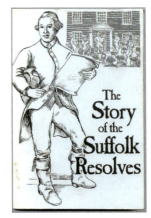

The Milton Historical Commission was formed in 1973 and it subsequently published "The Story of the Suffolk Resolves", written by Mary Webster and Charles Morris. The front cover, illustrated by Jack Coolidge, depicts Joseph Warren holding the Suffolk Resolves at the house of Daniel Vose in Milton Village, Massachusetts. Today, the house is known as the Suffolk Resolves House and serves as the home of the Milton Historical Society. The property is listed on the National Register of Historic Places. The Suffolk Resolves, primarily authored by Joseph Warren, is considered to be a foundational treatise to the Declaration of Independence.

away with all that superficial finery with which a corrupt Britain had disguised its designs on American liberty and dignity.

In addition to costume, Warren's stagecraft included a dramatic entry, though there is some dispute about the precise form of that entry. According to one account, he "ascended the Pulpit" from the front of the room, presumably passing through the crowd of soldiers who filled the aisles. According to another, he entered "from the rear by the pulpit window." And still another recalled that he climbed "a ladder at the pulpit window" (try doing that wearing a toga), to avoid pushing through the crowd of hostile soldiers. In any case, we can imagine this man, in his flowing toga, appearing before the packed audience like some kind of apparition. We can also imagine the hush that came over the boisterous crowd as its gaze fell upon the doctor. Before even uttering a word, his appearance would have spoken volumes to a crowd of Americans steeped in the virtues of ancient Rome.

As Warren began to speak, MacKenzie recalled, there were only a "few hisses from some of the officers." Samuel Adams similarly observed that Warren appeared to hold sway over the hostile members of the audience and another witness recalled that when one of the British officers [Capt. Chapman of the Welch Fusileers] held "up one of his hands in view of Warren, with several pistol bullets on the open palm," Warren silenced the officer by calmly dropping "a white handkerchief upon the officer's hand." It took true mastery of the orator's art form to turn so hostile a gesture to one's advantage. But Warren was obviously up to the task. Far from quieting his claims, the gesture gave the neo-Roman speaker an ideal chance to show that true virtue would be cowed by no threat of mere violence. Such was the way of the great Roman heroes of the day. The celebrated Roman politician Cato, for example, could take on the great and powerful Cæsar precisely because he was entirely immune to threats of violence. Virtue, in his lexicon, would always prevail over base power.

The gathering ended in disorder. After Warren stepped from the pulpit, Samuel Adams stood up and asked for a volunteer to deliver next year's commemorative oration. Adams apparently took the opportunity to reinforce colonists' sense that the events of 1770 represented an entirely unjust massacre. Not surprisingly, the redcoats, according to MacKenzie, "began to hiss," and someone mistakenly heard the words "Fire! Fire!" A scene of "the greatest confusion imaginable" ensued: amidst the screams of "fire" could be heard the threatening sounds of "drums & fifes of the 43rd regiment which happened to be passing by from exercise." According to another British witness, "the gallerians apprehending fire, bounded out of the windows, and swarmed down the gutters, like rats, into the street. The 43d regiment, returning accidentally from exercise, with drums beating, threw the whole body into the greatest consternation."

***

If the events surrounding the speech made for powerful political theater, what are we to make of the speech itself? The text, which was so widely reprinted, suggests that Warren skillfully blended the performative elements of his oration with the spoken elements.

Warren began with a historical account of early settlement, which was intended to "determine with what degree of justice the late parliament of Great Britain has assumed the power of giving away that property which the Americans have earned by their labour."

What followed was a Whig interpretation of colonial history. Warren portrayed a Manichean worldview in which "the tools of power in every age" confronted the benign power of liberty, embodied in his case by the Puritan forefathers. Those Puritans, "determined to find a place in which they might enjoy their freedom," exercised liberty in America through a charter obtained significantly from the British monarch rather than Parliament. They "cultivated and defended" the continent "at an infinite expense of toil and blood," and thus contributed vastly to the British Empire's greatness. Their serene prosperity, however, awakened "the madness of an avaricious minister" and brought about "the attempt of the British parliament to raise a revenue from America." These misfortunes "brought upon the stage discord, envy, hatred and revenge, with civil war close in their rear."

The speech, however, did not consist merely of a historical account of New England's settlement. Rather, Warren provided philosophical and ideological argument in defense of the colonists' position. "Personal freedom is the natural right of every man," he noted, as was the

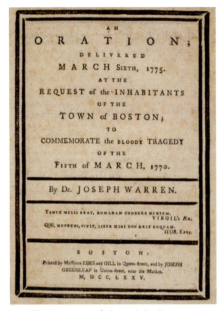

Front cover of the original paper pamphlet given to the inhabitants of the Town of Boston on March 6, 1775. Courtesy, American Antiquarian Society.

right to hold "what he has honestly acquired by his own labour" and to "pursue that course which is the most conducive" to happiness. Hence, "no man, or body of men, can without being guilty of flagrant injustice, claim a right to dispose of the persons or acquisitions of any other man". Warren continued with a celebration of the ancient Romans, who through self-effacing attitudes, "eminently conduced to the greatness of that state." We can only imagine what a difference it made to hear such classical musings from an orator clad in a toga.

***

Warren's Oration

"MY EVER HONOURED FELLOW CITIZENS, It is not without the most humiliating conviction of my want of ability that I now appear before you: but the sense I have of the obligation I am under to obey the calls of my country at all times, together with an animating recollection of your indulgence, exhibited upon so many occasions, has induced me, once more, undeserving as I am to throw myself upon that candour which looks with kindness on the feeblest efforts of an honest mind.

You will not now expect the elegance, the learning, the fire, the enrapturing strains of eloquence which charmed you when a LOVELL, a CHURCH, or a HANCOCK spake; but you will permit me to say that with sincerity, equal to theirs, I mourn over my bleeding country: with them I weep at her distress, and with them deeply resent the many injuries she has received from the hands of cruel and unreasonable men.

That personal freedom is the natural right of every man; and that property, or an exclusive right to dispose of what he has honestly acquired by his own labour, necessarily arises therefrom, are truths which common sense has placed beyond the reach of contradiction. And no man, or body of man, can without being guilty of flagrant injustice, claim a right to dispose of the persons or acquisitions of any other man, or body of men, unless it can be proved that such a right has arisen from some compact between the parties in which it has been explicitly and freely granted.

If I may be indulged in taking a retrospective view of the first settlement of our country, it will be easy to determine with what degree of justice the late parliament of Great Britain has assumed the power of giving away that property which the Americans have earned by their labour.

Our fathers having nobly resolved never to wear the yoke of despotism, and seeing the European world, at the time, through indolence and cowardice, falling a prey to tyranny, bravely threw themselves upon the bosom of the ocean, determined to find a place in which they might enjoy their freedom, or perish in the glorious attempt. Approving heaven beheld the favourite ark dancing upon the waves, and graciously preserved it until the chosen families were brought in safety to these western regions. They found the land swarming with savages, who threatened death with every kind of torture. But savages, and death with torture were far less terrible than slavery: nothing was so much the object of their abhorrence as a tyrant's power: they knew that it was more safe to dwell with man in his most unpolished state, -than in a country where arbitrary power prevails. Even anarchy itself, that bugbear held up by the tools of power (though truly to be deprecated) is infinitely less dangerous to mankind than arbitrary government. Anarchy can be but of short duration; for when men are at liberty to pursue that course which is most conducive to their own happiness, they will soon come into it, and from the rudest state of nature, order and good government must soon arise. But tyranny, when once established, entails its curses on a nation to the latest period of time; unless some daring genius, inspired by heaven, shall, unappalled danger, bravely form and execute the arduous design of restoring liberty and life to his enslaved, murdered country.

The tools of power, in every age, have racked their inventions to justify the few in sporting with the

happiness of the many; and, having found their sophistry too weak to hold mankind in bondage, have impiously dared to force religion, the daughter of the king of heaven, to become a prostitute in the service of hell. They taught that princes, honoured with the name of Christian, might bid defiance to the founder of their faith, might pillage Pagan countries and deluge them with blood, only because they boasted themselves to be the disciples of that teacher who strictly charged his followers to do to others as they would that others should do unto them.

This country, having been discovered by an English subject, in the year 1620, was (according to the system which the blind superstition of those times supported) deemed the property of the crown of England. Our ancestors, when they resolved to quit their native soil, obtained from King James, a grant of certain lands in North America. This they probably did to silence the cavils of their enemies, for it cannot be doubted but they despised the pretended right which he claimed thereto. Certain it is, that he might, with equal propriety and justice, have made them a grant of the planet Jupiter. And their subsequent conduct plainly shows that they were too well acquainted with humanity, and the principles of natural equity, to suppose that the grant gave them any right to take possession; they therefore entered into a treaty with the natives, and bought from them the lands: nor have I ever yet obtained any information that our ancestors ever pleaded, or that the natives ever regarded the grant from the English crown: the business was transacted by the parties in the same independent manner that it would have been, had neither of them ever known or heard of the island of Great Britain.

Having become the honest proprietors of the soil, they immediately applied themselves to the cultivation of it; and they soon held the virgin earth teeming with richest fruits, a grateful recompense for their unwearied toil. The fields began to wave with ripening harvests, and the late barren wilderness was seen to blossom like the rose. The savage natives saw with wonder the delightful change, and quickly formed a scheme to obtain that by fraud or force, which nature meant as the reward of industry alone. But the illustrious emigrants soon convinced the rude invaders, that they were not less ready to take the field for battle than for labour; and the insidious foe was driven from their borders as often as he ventured to disturb them. The crown of England looked with indifference on the contest; our ancestors were left alone to combat with the natives. Nor is there any reason to believe, that it ever was intended by the one party, or expected by the other, that the grantor should defend and maintain the grantees in the peaceable possession of the lands named in the patents. And it appears plainly, from the history of those times, that neither the prince, nor the people of England, thought themselves much interested in the matter. They had not then any idea of a thousandth part of those advantages which they since have, and we are most heartily willing they should still continue to reap from us.

But when, at an infinite expense of toil and blood, this widely extended continent had been cultivated and defended: when the hardy adventurers justly expected that they and their descendants should peaceably have enjoyed the harvest of those fields which they had sown, and the fruit of those vineyards which they had planted; this country was then thought worthy the attention of the British ministry; and the only justifiable and only successful means of rendering the colonies serviceable to Britain were adopted.

By an intercourse of friendly offices, the two countries became so united in affection, that they thought not of any distinct or separate interests, they found both countries flourishing and happy. Britain saw her commerce extended, and her wealth increased; her lands raised to an immense value; her fleets riding triumphant on the ocean; the terror of her arms spreading to every quarter of the globe. The colonist found himself free, and thought himself secure; he dwelt under his own vine, and under his own fig tree, and had none to make him afraid: he knew indeed that by purchasing the manufactures of Great Britain, he contributed to its greatness: he knew that all the wealth, that his labour produced centered in Great Britain; but that, far from exciting his envy, filled him with the highest pleasure; that thought supported him in all his toils. When the business of the day was past, he solaced himself with the contemplation, or perhaps entertained his listening family with the recital of some great, some glorious transaction which shines conspicuous in the history of Britain: or, perhaps, his elevated fancy led him to foretell with a kind of enthusiastic confidence, the glory, power, and duration of an empire which should extend from one end of the earth to the other: he saw, or thought he saw, the British nation risen to a pitch of grandeur which cast a veil over the Roman glory, and ravished with the preview, boasted a race of British kings, whose names should echo through those realms where Cyrus, Alexander, and the Cæsars were unknown; princes for whom millions of grateful subjects redeemed from slavery and Pagan ignorance, should, with thankful tongues, offer up their prayers and praises to that transcendently great and beneficent Being, by whom kings reign, and princes decree justice.

These pleasing connections might have continued; these delightsome prospects might have been every day extended; and even the reveries of the most warm imagination might have been realized; but unhappily for us, unhappily for Britain, the madness of an avaricious minister of state, has drawn a sable curtain over the charming scene, and in its stead, has brought upon the stage, discord, envy, hatred, and revenge, with civil war close in their rear.

Some demon, in an evil hour, suggested to a short sighted financier, the hateful project of transferring the whole property of the king's subjects in America, to his subjects in Britain. The claim of the British parliament to tax the colonies, can never be supported but by such a **TRANSFER**; for the right of the House of Commons of Great, Britain, to originate any tax, or grant money, is altogether derived from their being elected by the people of Great Britain to act for them; and the people of Great Britain cannot confer on their representatives a right to give or grant any thing which they themselves have not a right to give or grant personally.

***

Therefore it follows, that if the members chosen by the people of Great Britain, to represent them in parliament, have, by virtue of their being so chosen, any right to give or grant American property, or to lay any tax upon the lands or persons of the colonists, it is because the lands and people in the colonies are bonafide, owned by, and justly belonging to the people of Great Britain. But (As has been before observed) every man has a right to personal freedom, consequently a right to enjoy what is acquired by his own labour.

***

And as it is evident that the property in this country has been acquired by our own labour; it is the duty of the people of Great Britain, to produce some compact in which we have explicitly given up to them a right to dispose of our persons or property. Until this is done, every attempt of theirs, or of those whom they have deputed to act for them to give or grant

widowed mourner, here satiate thy grief; behold thy murdered husband gasping on the ground, and to complete the pompous show of wretchedness, bring in each hand thy infant children to bewail their father's fate. Take heed, ye orphan babes, lest, whilst your streaming eyes are fixed upon the ghastly corpse, your feet glide on the stones bespattered with your father's brains! Enough! this tragedy need not be heightened by an infant weltering in the blood of him that gave it birth. Nature, reluctant shrinks already from the view, and the chilled blood rolls slowly backward in its fountain. We wildly stare about, and with amazement, ask, who spread this ruin round us? what wretch has dared deface the image of his God? has haughty France, or cruel Spain, sent forth her myrmidons? has the grim savage rused again from the far distant wilderness? or does some fiend, fierce from the depth of hell, with all the rancorous malice, which the apostate damned can feel, twang her destructive bow, and hurl her deadly arrows at our breast? no, none of these; but, how astonishing! It is the hand of Britain that inflicts the wound. The arms of George, our rightful king, have been employed to shed that blood, when justice, or the honour of his crown, had called his subjects to the field.

But pity, grief, astonishment, with all the softer movements of the soul, must now give way to stronger passions. Say, fellow citizens, what dreadful thought now swells your heaving bosoms; you fly to arms, sharp indignation flashes from each eye, revenge gnashes her iron teeth, death grins an hideous smile, secure to drench his greedy jaws in human gore, whilst hovering furies darken all the air.

But stop, my bold adventurous countrymen, stain not your weapons with the blood of Britons. Attend to reason's voice, humanity puts in her claim, and sues to be again admitted to her wonted seat, the bosom of the brave. Revenge is far beneath the noble mind. Many perhaps, compelled to rank among the vile assassins, do, from their inmost souls, detest the barbarous action. The winged death, shot from your arms, may chance to pierce some breast that bleeds already for your injured country.

The storm subsides; a solemn pause ensues; you spare, upon condition they depart. They go; they quit your city; they no more shall give offence. Thus closes the important drama.

And could it have been convinced that we again should have seen a British army in our land, sent to enforce obedience to acts of parliament destructive of our liberty. But the royal ear, far distant from this western world, has been assaulted by the tongue of slander; and villains, traitorous alike to king and country, have prevailed upon a gracious prince to clothe his countenance with wrath, and to erect the hostile banner against a people ever affectionate and loyal to him his illustrious predecessors of the house of Hanover.

***

Our streets are again filled with armed men; our harbour is crowded with ships of war; but these cannot intimidate us; our liberty must be preserved; it is far dearer than life, we hold it even dear as our allegiance; we must defend it against the attacks of friends as well as enemies; we cannot suffer even Britons to ravish it from us.

***

No longer could we reflect, with generous pride, or the heroic actions of our American forefathers, no longer boast our origin from that far famed island, whose warlike sons have so often drawn their well tried swords to save her from the ravages of tyranny; could we, but for a moment, entertain the thought of giving up our liberty. The man who meanly will submit to wear a shackle, contemns the noblest gift of heaven, and impiously affronts the God that made him free.

It was a maxim of the Roman people, which eminently conduced to the greatness of that state, never to despair of the commonwealth. The maxim may prove as salutary to us now, as it did to them. Short sighted mortals see not the numerous links of small and great events, which form the chain on which the fate of kings and nations is suspended. Ease and prosperity (though pleasing for a day) have often sunk a people into effeminacy and sloth. Hardships and dangers (though we for ever strive to shun them) have frequently called forth such virtues, as have commanded the applause and reverence of an admiring world. Our country loudly calls you to be circumspect, vigilant, active, and brave. Perhaps (all gracious Heaven avert it) perhaps, the power of Britain, a nation great in war, by some malignant influence, may be employed to enslave you: but let not even this discourage you. Her arms it is true, have filled the world with terror; her troops have reaped the laurels of the field: her fleets have rode triumphant on the sea–and when, or where, did you, my countrymen, depart inglorious from the field of fight?2 You too can shew the trophies of your forefathers victories and your own; can name the fortresses and battles you have won; and many of you count the honourable scars or wounds received while fighting for your king and country.

Where justice is the standard, heaven is the warrior's shield; but conscious guilt unnerves the arm that lifts the sword against the innocent. Britain, united with these colonies, by commerce and affection, by interest and blood, may mock the threats of France and Spain; may be the, seat of universal empire. But should America, either by force, or those more dangerous engines, luxury and corruption, ever be brought into a state of vassalage, Britain must lose her freedom Also. No longer shall she sit the empress of the sea: her ships no more shall waft her thunders over the wide ocean: the wreath shall wither on her temples: her weakened arm shall be unable to defend her coasts: and she, at last, must bow her venerable head to some proud foreigner's despotic rule.

But, if from past events, we may venture to form a judgment of the future, we justly may expect that the devices of our enemies will but increase the triumphs of our country. I must indulge a hope that Britain's liberty, as well as ours, will eventually be preserved by the virtue of America.

***

The attempt of the British parliament to raise a revenue from America, and our denial of their right to do it, have excited an almost universal inquiry into the rights of mankind in general, and of British subjects in particular; the necessary result of which must be such a liberality of sentiment, and such a jealousy of those in power, as will, better than an adamantine wall, secure us against the future approaches of despotism.

***

The malice of the Boston port bill has been defeated in a very considerable degree, by giving you an opportunity of deserving, and our brethren in this and our sister colonies an opportunity of bestowing, those benefactions which have delighted your friends and astonished your enemies, not only in America, but in Europe also. And what is more valuable still, the sympathetic feelings for a brother is distress, and the grateful emotions excited in the breast of him who finds relief, must for ever endear each other, and form those indissoluble bonds of friendship and affection, on which the preservation of our rights so evidently depend.

The mutilation of our charter has made every other colony jealous for its own; for this, if once submitted to us, would get on float the property and government of every British settlement upon the continent. If charters are not deemed sacred, how miserably precarious is every thing founded upon them.

Even the sending troops to put these acts in execution, is not without advantages to us. The exactness and beauty of their discipline inspire our youth with ardour in the pursuit of military knowledge. Charles the invincible, taught Peter the Great, the art of war. The battle of Pultowa convinced Charles of the proficiency Peter had made.

***

Our country is in danger, but not to be despaired of. Our enemies are numerous and powerful; but we have many friends, determining to be free, and heaven and earth will aid the resolution. On you depend the fortunes of America. You are to decide the important question, on which rest the happiness and liberty of millions yet unborn. Act worthy of yourselves.

***

The faltering tongue of hoary age calls on you to support your country. The lisping infant raises its suppliant hands, imploring defence against the monster slavery. Your fathers look from their celestial seats with smiling approbation on their sons, who boldly stand forth in the cause of virtue; but sternly frown upon the inhuman miscreant, who, to secure the loaves and fishes to himself, would breed a serpent to destroy his children.

But, pardon me, my fellow citizens, I know you want not zeal or fortitude. You will maintain your rights or perish in the generous struggle. However, difficult the combat, you never will decline it when freedom is the prize. An independence on Great Britain is not our aim. No, our wish is, that Britain and the colonies may, like the oak and the ivy, grow and increase in strength together. But whilst the infatuated plan or making one part of the empire slaves to the other, is persisted in; the interest and safety of Britain, as well as the colonies, require that the wise measures, recommended by the honourable the continental congress, be steadily pursued; whereby the unnatural contest between a parent honoured, and a child beloved, may probably be brought to such an issue, as that the peace and happiness of both may be established upon a lasting basis. But if these pacific measures are ineffectual, and it appears that the only way to safety, is through fields of blood, I know you will not turn your faces from your foes, but will, undauntedly, press forward, until tyranny is trodden under foot, and you have fixed your adored goddess Liberty, fast by a Brunswick's side, on the American throne.

You then, who nobly have espoused your country's cause, who generously have sacrificed wealth and ease; who had despised the pomp and shew of tinseled greatness; refused the summons to the festive board; been deaf to the alluring calls of luxury and mirth; who have forsaken the downy pillow to keep your vigils by the midnight lamp, for the salvation of your invaded county, that you might break the fowler's snare, and disappoint the vulture of his prey, you then will reap that harvest of renown which you so justly have deserved. Your country shall pay her grateful tribute of applause. Even the children of your most inveterate enemies, ashamed to tell from whom they sprang, while they in secret, curse their stupid, cruel parents, shall join the general voice of gratitude to those who broke the fetters which their fathers forged.

Having redeemed your country, and secured the blessing to future generations, who, fired by your example, shall emulate your virtues, and learn from you the heavenly art of making millions happy; with heart felt joy, which transports all your own, you cry, the glorious work is done. Then drop the mantle to some young Elisha, and take your seats with kindred spirits in your native skies.

Finis

How the War Began: The Siege at Boston (cont'd)

The efforts of the patriots to keep off the issue were met, almost of course in a garrison-town, by the outrages of irresponsible soldiers. Every act of violence by them was, of course, put on record immediately. Here is a letter dated on the 12th of March:

March 12, 1775.

An honest countryman, Thomas Ditson of Billerica, was inquiring on Wednesday for a firelock. A soldier heard him, and told him he had one he would sell. Away goes the ignoramus, and after paying the soldier very honestly for the gun, which was only an old one without a lock, was walking off, when half a dozen seized him, and hurried the poor fellow away, under guard, for breach of the act against trading with the soldiers; and, after keeping him in duress all night, the next morning, instead of carrying him before a magistrate, who, on complaint, would have fined him, as has been the case in several instances, the officers condemned the man, without a hearing, to be tarred and feathered, which was accordingly executed. After stripping him naked, and covering him with tar and feathers, they mounted him upon a one-horse truck, and surrounding it with a guard of twenty soldiers with fixed bayonets, accompanied with all the drums and fifes of the regiment (Forty-seventh), and a number of officers, negroes, sailors, &c., exhibited him as a spectacle through the principal streets of the town. They fixed a label on his back, on which was written, "American Liberty, or a specimen of Democracy;" and, to add to the insult, they played "Yankee Doodle."

"O Britain! how art thou fallen!"

What a wretched figure will the Boston expedition hereafter make on the historic page!

The Billerica selectmen remonstrated to Gen. Gage in a well-written paper, which ends with ominous words: —

"May it please your Excellency, we must tell you we are determined, if the innocent inhabitants of our country towns must be interrupted by soldiers in their lawful intercourse with the town of Boston, and treated with the most brutish ferocity, we shall hereafter use a different style from that of petition and complaint."

No. 3 of "The Crisis," an anonymous political pamphlet of the time, seemed too violent to be borne; and each House ordered that it should be burned by the hangman. Here is the description of the cremation: [1]

"To THE King.

"Sir, — To follow you regularly through every step of a fourteen-years' shameful and inglorious reign would be a task as painful as disagreeable, and far exceed the bounds of this paper. But we are called upon by the necessity of the times, the measures you are pursuing, by every principle of justice and self-preservation, and by the duty we owe to God and our country, to declare our sentiments (with a freedom becoming Englishmen) in some of those dreadful transactions and oppressions which the kingdom has labored under since the glory and luster of England's crown was doomed to fade upon your brow, and to point out to you, sir, your own critical and dangerous situation.

"Sir, it is not your rotten troop in the present House of Commons; it is not your venal, beggarly, pensioned Lords; it is not your polluted, canting, prostituted Bench of Bishops; it is not your whole set of abandoned ministers ; nor your army of Scotch cut-throats, — that can protect you from the people's rage, when driven by your oppressions, and, until now, unheard-of cruelties, to a state of desperation."

The temper of London may be judged from the fact that John Wilkes was mayor. He had very little question about what was coming, and as little question about proclaiming it. On the 7th of February, on Lord North's resolution for an address to the king to shut the Colonies out from the fisheries, Wilkes made a speech, which was printed in full in the Boston papers at the end of March. He closed in these prophetic words: —

"Sir, this address is founded in injustice and cruelty. It is equally contrary to the sound maxims of true policy, and to the unerring rule of natural right. The Americans will defend their property and their liberties with the spirit of freemen, with the spirit I hope we should. They will sooner declare themselves independent, and risk every consequence of such a contest, than submit to the yoke which administration is preparing for them. An address of so sanguinary a nature cannot fail of driving them to despair. They will see that you are preparing not only to draw the sword, but to burn the scabbard. You

---

[1] "Yesterday (March 6), No. 3 of ' The Crisis,' and a pamphlet with the same title, containing thoughts on American affairs, were burnt by the common hangman at Westminster Hall gate, pursuant to a unanimous order of the Houses of Lords and Commons. As soon as the condemned papers were burnt, a man threw into the fire. The Address of both Houses of Parliament to his Majesty, declaring the Bostonians in Actual Rebellion,' likewise * The Address of the Bishops and Clergy assembled in Convocation.' The sheriffs were much hissed for attending; and the populace diverted themselves with throwing the fire at each other.
"And this day, at twelve o'clock, the sheriffs attended at the Royal Exchange for the above purpose; but, as soon as the fire was lighted, it was put out, and dead dogs and cats thrown at the officers. A fire was then made in Cornhill ; and the executioner did his duty. Sheriff Haft was wounded in the wrist and Sheriff Plumer in the breast, by a brickbat. Mr. Gates, the city marshal, was dismounted, and with much difficulty saved his life."
This is the beginning, and perhaps worst passage in "The Crisis," No. 3. Whatever vehemence came into the American literature is certainly quite matched by their London brethren. It has proved to be quite true.

are declaring them rebels. Every idea of reconciliation will vanish. They will pursue the most rigorous measures in their own defense. The whole continent will be dismembered from Great Britain, and the wide arch of the raised empire fall. But I hope the just vengeance of the people will overtake the author of the pernicious counsels, and the loss of the first province of the empire be speedily followed by the loss of the heads of those ministers who advised these wicked and fatal measures."

PART FIVE
THE MARCH UPON LEXINGTON AND CONCORD

Centennial Publication: *One Hundred Years Ago: How the War Began* by Edward Hale

Engraving by Amos Doolittle (1754-1832) titled "The Battle of Lexington".

> *"On the nineteenth day of April, one thousand seven hundred and seventy-five, a day to be remembered by all Americans of the present generation, and which ought, and doubtless will be handed down to ages yet unborn, the troops of Britain, unprovoked, shed the blood of sundry of the loyal American subjects of the British king in the field of Lexington."*

These words are the prophetic introduction of the "Narrative of the Excursion of the King's Troops under the Command of Gen. Gage," which the Provincial Congress of Massachusetts sent to England a hundred years ago. With infinite care the Congress drew up depositions, which were sworn to before "his Majesty's justices of the peace," that, with all legal form, they might show to all the world who were the aggressors, now the crisis had come. Then they entrusted the precious volume of these depositions to Richard Derby of Salem, who sent John Derby with them to England. The vessel made a good run. She arrived on the 29th of May with the official papers and "The Essex Gazette," which had the published accounts. "The Sukey," Capt. Brown, with the government accounts, forwarded by Gen. Gage, did not arrive till eleven days after. Meanwhile, Arthur Lee and all the friends of America in London were steadily publishing the news of the "ministerial" attack on the people, and the people's repulse of the army. The public charged the government with concealing the news. Thus was it, that, when they told their own story."

> *"The embattled farmers stood, and fired the shot heard round the world,"*

All parties had had fair notice that the crisis was coming; and they had a good chance to guess how it was coming. On the 30th of March, by way of seeing how people would bear the presence of an army, and how the army would march after a winter's rest and rust, Earl Percy with five regiments marched out over Boston Neck, into the country. Boston people can trace him by walking out on Washington Street, where the sea-water then flowed on both sides, up the hill at Roxbury, on the right of the church, and heeding Gov. Dudley's parting-stone, which still stands, let them take Centre Street, "to Dedham and Rhode Island." Along that road to Jamaica Plain, Earl Percy marched, his drums and fifes playing "Yankee Doodle." The spring was very early. Some soldiers straggled, and trampled down gardens and fields that were planted, perhaps since last fall. From Jamaica Plain, Earl Percy led them across to Dorchester; and by the Dorchester road they came home. Very indignant was the Provincial Congress and the committees of safety at this first "invasion" of the country; and all people guessed that Concord would be the point of the next "excursion," because at Concord was one of the largest deposits of stores which the Province of Massachusetts had collected in its preparations against the British empire. What these preparations were, we will try to tell on the next page.

As early as Feb. 9, the Provincial Congress had intimated their intention of stopping such "excursions." They had appointed the celebrated "Committee of Safety," with the express purpose of checking them. Of this committee, —

> *"The business and duty it shall be, most carefully and diligently to inspect and observe all and every such person or persons as shall at any time attempt to carry into*

execution, by force, an act of the British parliament, entitled 'An Act for the Better Regulating the Government of the Province of Massachusetts Bay, in New England' ... which said committee, or any five of them, provided always that not more than one of the said five shall be an inhabitant of the town of Boston, shall have power, and they are hereby empowered and directed, when they shall judge that such attempt or attempts are made, to alarm, muster, and cause to be assembled with the utmost expedition, and completely armed, accoutred, and supplied with provisions sufficient for their support in their march to the place of rendezvous, such and so many of the militia of this Province as they shall judge necessary for the end and purpose of opposing such attempt or attempts, and at such place or places as they shall judge proper, and them to discharge as the safety of the Province shall permit."

This, it will be observed, was full preparation for war, only the Provincial Congress meant that Gen. Gage should strike the first blow. Meanwhile, our friends Bernicre and Brown, whose sad tramp to Worcester we traced in the last number of Old and New, were sent to see what there was at Concord. They left their journal behind them, when, the next year, the English army evacuated Boston; and so we are able to trace their march today.

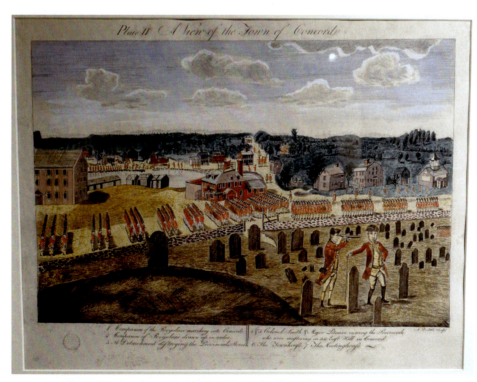

Engraving by Amos Doolittle titled "A View of the Town of Concord" depicts the British entering concord.

And so it happened that on the evening of the 18th of April, when, it was supposed, most of the Boston people were in bed, about eight hundred soldiers — grenadiers, light-infantry, and marines — were embarked in the boats of the navy, very near the place where the Old Providence Station stood, where then the tide rose and fell. Remember that there was no bridge at that time from Boston on any side. The little army was ferried across to Lechmere's Point, not far from the Court House of today ; lost two hours in going so far, and then took up its silent line of march through Cambridge, by what is still remembered as Milk Row. At the tavern in Menotomy, now West Cambridge, the rebel committee of safety had been in session the day before. Dear Old Gen. Heath, then only "our colonel," whose memoirs come in in the most entertaining reading of the time, had been there. But he had gone home to Roxbury. Here is his account of what happened to those who said: —

"*On the 19th, at daybreak, our general was awoke, called from his bed, and informed that a detachment of the British army were out, that they had crossed from Boston to Phipps's Farm in boats, and had gone towards Concord, as was supposed, with intent to destroy the public stores. They probably had notice that the committees had met the preceding day at Wetherby's Tavern, at Menotomy; for, when they came opposite to the house, they halted. Several of the gentlemen slept there during the night. Among them were Col. Orne, Col. Lee, and Mr. Gerry. One of them awoke, and informed the others that a body of the British were before the house. They immediately made their escape, without time to dress themselves, at the backdoor, receiving some injury from obstacles in the way, in their undressed state. They made their way into the fields.*"

Heath had met on his way home officers who tried to keep the news of the "excursion" from reaching Concord; but the country was alarmed, and Col. Smith sent back to Boston for a re-enforcement. Gen. Gage had expected the request, and had ordered the first brigade under arms at four that morning. These orders were carried to the first brigade-major's. He was not at home; and, when he came home, his servant forgot to tell of the letter. At four o'clock no brigade appeared. At five o'clock Col. Smith's express came, asking the re-enforcement. On inquiry, it proved that no orders were given; and it was not till six that a part of the brigade paraded. They waited till seven for the marines. Is not all this like a village muster today? At seven, there being still no marines, it proved that the order for them had been addressed to Major Pitcairn, who was by this time far away, and had indeed begun the war already, without knowing it, by firing his pistol on Lexington Common. So the half of the brigade waited, and waited, till the marines could he got ready', and when they were ready, at nine o'clock, started over Boston Neck ; for now they had no boats : so that they must even go six miles round by land, as every Bostonian will see. So they came to Dudley's parting-stone, playing" Yankee Doodle" again; but, when they reached the stone this time, they took the right-hand road" to Cambridge and Watertown." A Roxbury boy who sat on a stone wall to see them pass prophesied thus to Percy, referring to the history of his noble house, —"You go out by ' Yankee Doodle; ' but you will come back by 'Chevy Chase.' "While the half-brigade was waiting for the marines on what is now Tremont Street, its line crossing the head of Beacon Street, a little boy nine year's old, named Harrison Gray Otis, was on his way to the old school in School Street, where Parker's stands to-day. Here is his account of it, printed for the first time. It is, so far as we know, the only glimpse we have of Boston life on that memorable day.

"*On the 10th April, 1775, I went to school for the last time. In the morning, about seven, Piercy's brigade was drawn up, extending from Scollay's buildings, through Tremont Street, and nearly to the bottom of the mall, preparing to take*

Engraving by Amos Doolittle "The Engagement at the North Bridge in Concord", known as Plate III of a four colored engravings that were Doolittle's largest commercial success in folk art depictions.

up their march for Lexington. A corporal came up to me as I was going to school, and turned me off, to pass down Court Street; which I did, and came up School Street to the schoolhouse. It may well be imagined that great agitation prevailed, the British line being drawn up four yards only from the schoolhouse-door. As I entered school, I heard the announcement of 'deponite libros,' and ran home for fear of the regulars. Here ended my connection with Mr. Lovell's administration of the school. Soon afterwards I left town, and did not return until after the evacuation by the British, in March, 1776."

Col. Smith and his eight hundred had pressed on meanwhile. The alarm had been so thoroughly given in Lexington, that, at two o'clock, the militia had assembled (one hundred and thirty in number) ; and John Parker, their captain, had ordered them to load with powder and ball. This John is the grandfather of one Theodore, who will appear two generations afterwards. No sign of any troops; and the men were dismissed, with orders to assemble again at the beat of drum. Most of them thought that the whole was a false alarm. But Gage's officers, in the advance of the English column, came back to it on its march, and reported that five hundred men were in arms. Major Pitcairn of the marines had command of six companies of light infantry in advance. He caught all of Parker's scouts, except Thaddeus Bowman, who galloped back to Lexington Common, and gave to Parker tidings of the approach of the column.

Parker ordered the drum to beat; and his men began to collect. He ordered Sergeant William Monroe to form them in two ranks, a few rods north of the meeting-house. The English officers, hearing the drum, halted their troops, bade them prime and load, and then marched forward at double-quick. Sixty or seventy of the militia had assembled. The tradition is, that Parker had bidden the men not fire till they were fired upon, but added, "If they mean to have a war, let it begin here." Double-quick on one side; on the other, Sergeant Monroe forming his men as well as he can. Major Pitcairn is in the advance. "Ye villains, ye rebels, disperse! Lay down your arms! Why don't ye lay down your arms? "He saw a gun flash in the pan. The men did not disperse. Pitcairn declared, till the day he died at Bunker Hill, that he gave no order to fire, that he commanded not to fire; and it seems to be admitted that he stuck his staff or sword downward, as the signal to forbear firing. But some men in his party fired irregularly, and hurt no one. Then came a general discharge from the English line, and many men were killed or wounded. The militia returned the fire, — some before leaving their line, some after, — and the war was begun.

Here is Capt. John Parker's account of the fight, one of the papers which Capt. Derby carried to London: —

"I, John Parker, of lawful age, and commander of the militia at Lexington, do testify and declare, that on the nineteenth instant, in the morning, about one of the clock, being informed that there were a number of the regular officers riding up and down the road, stopping and insulting people as they passed the road, and also informed that a number of the regular troops were on their march from Boston, in order to take the Province stores at Concord, I ordered our militia to meet on the common in said Lexington, to consult what to do ; and concluded not to be discovered, nor

meddle, or make with said regular troops, if they should approach, unless they should insult or molest us ; and, upon their sudden approach, I immediately ordered our militia to disperse, and not to fire. Immediately said troops made their appearance, and, rushing furiously on, fired upon and killed eight of our party, without receiving any provocation therefor from us."

'Middlesex ss., April 25, 1775.

'The above-named John Parker personally appeared, and, after being duly cautioned to tell the whole truth, made solemn oath to the truth of the above deposition by him subscribed before us.

William Reed.
Joshua Johnson.
William Stickney.
Justices of the Peace."

Engraving by Amos Doolittle, "A View of the South Part of Lexington" depicts the British retreating from Lexington". Doolittle's accounts are taken from his visual survey of the actual scenes in 1775.

That is the way those people went to war. They fought one day; and then they made depositions to secure the truth of history. Henry Clay was greatly amused when a New-England historian told him of these depositions. He heard the story in some detail, and then said, "Tell me that again."

But they did not stop for depositions then. The militia retired: some here, some there. The English troops fired a volley on the common, and gave three cheers. Col. Smith came up with the main party; and they all pressed on to Concord. Two of their party had been wounded. Major Pitcairn's horse was struck by a ball; and, after the column left Lexington, six of the regulars were taken prisoners. The musket of one of them is in the State House to-day.

Meanwhile the Concord militia had the alarm, and had formed. The minute-men, and some of the militia from Lincoln, the next town, had joined them. Some of the companies marched down the Lexington road till they saw the approaching column. They saw they were outnumbered; and they fell back to a hill, about eighty rods distance back of the town, where they formed. Col. Barrett, their commander, joined them here. He had been at work that day, executing such commands as these, given by the committee of safety the day before. They are worth looking back upon as illustrations of the preparations of these days.

"*April* 18, 1775.

"*Voted, That part of the provisions be removed from Concord; viz., fifty barrels of beef from thence to Sudbury, with Deacon Plympton, a hundred barrels of flour (of which what is in the malt-house in Concord be part), twenty casks of rice, fifteen hogsheads of molasses, ten hogsheads of rum, five hundred candles.*

"*Voted, That the musket-balls under the care of Col. Barrett be buried under ground in some safe place; that he be desired to do it, and to let the commissary only be informed thereof.*"

Still finding himself outnumbered. Col. Barrett then withdrew his force over the North Bridge; and the little English army marched into the town.

Three of their companies were stationed at the bridge: three companies were sent to Col. Barrett's house, two miles distant, to destroy the magazines. Did they find the musket-bullets? No. Another party was sent to the South Bridge. In the centre of the town they broke off the trunnions of three new cannon, destroyed what stores they could find, among others some wooden spoons and trenchers, which appear quite conspicuously in all the accounts. But from all such work all parties were called by firing at the bridge.

All this time, the minute-men had been pouring in on the high grounds where Col. Barrett had formed his men. They saw at last that the troops had fired the town, in one place and another. The court-house was on fire. Capt. William Smith of Lincoln volunteered to take his company, and dislodge the guard at the bridge. Isaac Davis, of the Acton company, made the remark, which has become a proverb, " There is not a man of my company that is afraid " to go. Col. Barrett ordered the attack, bade the column pass the bridge, but not to fire unless they were fired upon. Again the passion for law appeared: "It is the king's highway; and we have a right to march upon it, if we march to Boston. , Forward, march!" They marched to the air of "the White Cockade," the quickest step their fifes could play.

Laurie, in command of the English party, crossed back on the bridge, and began to take up the planks. Major Buttrick, who commanded the attacking party, hurried his men. When they were within a few rods, the English fired, in three several discharges. Mr. Emerson, the minister of Concord (who, also, will appear two generations afterwards), came nearer the soldiers than those that were killed. Three several discharges were made by the English; and Mr. Emerson" was very uneasy till the fire was returned." Isaac Davis and Abner Hosmer were killed; and then Major Buttrick gave the order to fire. The English retired. The Provincials crossed the bridge, and part of them ascended the bold hill, which visitors to Concord remember, behind the meeting-house, on the right of the town. The English party under Parsons returned from Barrett's, and crossed the bridge again; but they were left to join the main body without offence.

One English soldier had been killed, and several wounded. Col. Smith delayed his return till he could find carriages for his wounded; and it was noon before he began his return. Meanwhile, north and south and west, couriers had been speeding, announcing that the Lexington militia had been fired on. The minute-men, the country through, had started on their march. They did not know what point to strike. They did not know what they were to do when they came there. But they marched: they were determined to be in time; and in time they were. The populous country between Boston and Con- cord was in arms. The men knew every inch of ground, and, after they had had their shot at the regulars in one place, ran across country, and tried them again in another. "They are trained to protect themselves behind stone walls," wrote Gen. Gage to the ministry

"They seemed to drop from the clouds," says an English soldier. Poor Smith and his party, after thirty miles of tramping, came back to Lexington Common, in no mood for giving three huzzas there. They made quick marching of it, and were there by two. They left Concord at noon.

"*A number of our officers were wounded,*" *says Bernicre ;* " *so that we began to- run rather than retreat in order. The whole behaved with amazing bravery, but little order.*"

Here Percy met them with his Late re-enforcement here they rested, and then resumed the retreat, to receive just the same treatment in every defile. At West Cambridge, the Danvers company, observe Danvers again, — the flank company of the Essex regiment, had come up. Fifteen miles they had marched in four hours, across Essex County. It was sunset before the head of what column was left crossed Charlestown Neck. All Boston was on Beacon Hill, watching for their return. Through the gathering twilight, men could see from the hill the flashes of the muskets on Milk Row ; and Percy had to unlimber his field-pieces, and bring them into use again. It was at West Cambridge that Dr. Warren so exposed himself, that a pin was struck out of the hair of his earlock. Heath was by this time exercising some sort of command. The head of the English column was at Bunker Hill, when an aide of Pickering's rode up to him, to announce that the Essex regiment was close behind him. Danvers had gone across country : the rest of the regiment had marched direct to Boston. Heath

any part of our property, is directly repugnant to every principle of reason and natural justice. But, I may boldly say, that such a compact never existed, no, not even in imagination. Nevertheless, the representatives of a nation, long famed for justice and the exercise of every noble virtue, have been prevailed on to adopt the fatal scheme: and although the dreadful consequences of this wicked policy have already shaken the empire to its centre; yet still it is persisted in. Regardless of the voice of reason, deaf to the prayers and supplications, and unaffected with the flowing tears of suffering millions, the British ministry still hug the darling idol; and every rolling year affords fresh instances of the absurd devotion with which they worship it. Alas! how has the folly, the distraction of the British councils, blasted our swelling hopes, and spread a gloom over this western hemisphere.

The hearts of Britons and Americans, which lately felt the generous glow of mutual confidence and love, now burn with jealousy and rage. Though, but of yesterday, I recollect (deeply affected at the ill boding change) the happy hours that past whilst Britain and America rejoiced in the prosperity and greatness of each other (heaven grant those halcyon days may soon return.) But now the Briton too often looks on the American with an envious eye taught to consider his just plea for the enjoyment of his earnings, as the effect of pride and stubborn opposition to the parent country. Whilst the American beholds the Briton as the ruffian, ready first to take away his property, and next, what is still dearer to every virtuous man, the liberty of his country.

When the measures of administration had disgusted the colonies to the highest degree, and the people of Great Britain had, by artifice and falsehood, been irritated against America, an army was sent over to enforce submission to certain acts of the British parliament, which reason scorned to countenance, and which placemen and pensioners were found unable to support.

Martial law and the government of a well regulated city, are so entirely different, that it has always been considered as improper to quarter troops in populous cities; frequent disputes must necessarily arise between the citizen and the soldier, even if no previous animosities subsist. And it is further certain, from a consideration of the nature of mankind, as well as from constant experience, that standing armies always endanger the liberty of the subject. But when the people on the one part, considered the army as sent to enslave them, and the army on the other, were taught to look on the people as in a state of rebellion, it was but just to fear the most disagreeable consequences. Our fears, we have seen, were but too well grounded.

***

The many injuries offered to the town, I pass over in silence. I cannot now mark out the path which led to that unequaled scene of horror, the sad remembrance of which, takes the full possession of my soul. The sanguinary theatre again opens itself to view. The baleful images of terror crowd around me, and discontented ghosts, with hollow groans, appear to solemnize the anniversary of the FIFTH of MARCH.

***

Approach we then the melancholy walk of death. Hither let me call the gay companion; here let him drop a farewell tear upon that body which so late he saw vigorous and warm with social mirth; hither let me lead the tender mother to weep over her beloved son: come

judged that it was too late for any further attack. The English, on their side, planted sentries at the Neck. Heath planted them on the other side, and ordered the militia to lie on their arms at Cambridge.

But, long before this time, the news of the march had travelled north and west and south. The memory of the rider "on the white horse" is still told in tradition, reminding one, as Gov. Washburn has said, of the white horse in the Revelation. The march and retreat were on Wednesday. On Sunday morning they had a rumor of it in New York; and on Tuesday they had a second express from New England with quite a connected story. This story was so definite, that they ventured to send it south by express as they received it from New Haven. To Elizabethtown, to Woodbridge, to New Brunswick, to Princeton, it flew as fast as horse could carry it.

The indorsements by the different committees show their eager haste. It was in Baltimore on the 27th. It was in Georgetown, S.C., on the 10th of May.

It told how the king's troops were besieged on Winter Hill; how Lord Percy was killed, and another general officer of the English, on the first fire. "To counterbalance this good news, the story is, that our first man in command (who he is, I know not) is also killed." No man since has known who "our first man in command" was. There was no commander all day long.

The dispatch was all untrue. But it told of war, and it fired the whole country. On the 20th of April an army was around Boston, and the siege had begun.

***

Here is the circular which the Committee of Safety sent to every town in Massachusetts, on the morning after the "battle of Lexington "and" Concord fight."

"Gentlemen, — The barbarous murders committed on our innocent brethren, on Wednesday the 19th instant, have made it absolutely necessary that we immediately raise an army to defend om- wives and our children from the butchering hands of an inhuman soldiery, who, incensed at the obstacles they met with in their bloody progress, and enraged at being repulsed from the field of slaughter, will, without the least doubt, take the first opportunity in their power to ravage this devoted country with fire and sword. We conjure you, therefore, by all that is dear, by all that is sacred, that you give all assistance possible in forming an army. Our all is at stake. Death and devastation are the instant consequences of delay. Every moment is infinitely precious. An hour lost may deluge your country in blood, and entail perpetual slavery upon the few of your posterity who may survive the carnage. We beg and entreat, as you will answer to your country, to your own consciences, and, above all, as you will answer to God himself, that you will hasten and encourage, by all possible means, the enlistment of men to form the army, and send them forward to headquarters at Cambridge, with that expedition which the vast importance and instant urgency of the affair demand."

***

This circular was written by Dr. Warren, who for sixty days had acted as the chairman of the Committee of Safety of Massachusetts, and represented the State, not to say the united colonies, — and represented them with intense fire, untiring energy, and solid good sense. What might have been, who shall tell? But the little bit which we have of a revelation of Warren's abilities, leads one to recur to the impression of the time. There was, so far as can be seen, a popular enthusiasm for Warren, such as no other leader commanded. Probably no reader will carefully read his letters and speeches without falling in with the estimate which the impulsive men of his time formed of him, — that here was a leader wholly worthy of the cause.

The minute-men staid for a few days at Cambridge and at Roxbury. By the 24th of April, Gen. Artemas Ward, who was in command, began to be uneasy because so many of them were returning home; and he urged the Provincial Congress, which had assembled by this time, to hurry their preparations for enlisting an army, and to let him have, on that day, his orders for the enlistment. The Congress had, on the day before, which was Sunday, voted that an army of thirty thousand was necessary. Meanwhile, Gen. Gage had had enough of "excursions;" and what is popularly called the "Siege of Boston" began with the 20th of April. A letter of the 26th, from Dr. Warren to him, makes the first suggestion for the removal from the town of its inhabitants. To this Gage agreed, on condition that they should surrender their arm; and a large number of fire-arms were surrendered on the 27th of April at Faneuil Hall. The enumeration is enough to show the military habit of the time. There were "seventeen hundred and seventy-eight fire-arms, six hundred and thirty-four pistols, nine hundred and seventy-three bayonets, and thirty-eight blunderbusses," — a very large supply for a town of seventeen thousand people, had they not been a people accustomed to count one-fifth of their population "fighting men," if we may borrow the words which Mrs. Child put into the mouth of James Otis.

Thomas Gage, the unfortunate pivot on which turned the fate of the English empire at this moment, was, as need hardly be said, the younger son of an English nobleman. The eternal laws asserted themselves all through this business. And, because England was governed by an aristocracy, it happened that George Sackville, who had been cashiered for cowardice, was now secretary for the colonies; that Sir John Burgoyne was on his way to re-enforce Gage; and that Gage, being second son of Viscount Gage, was in command. He first appears in our history as an aide of Braddock's; and he and George Washington served together in that campaign. He married in New York one of the Kembles of New Jersey; he was with Wolfe at Quebec; he was colonel of the Twenty-second Regiment of foot, and, as he knew America, was selected to be the military governor to whom the English Government entrusted its plans.

Gage at first assented to the proposal that the inhabitants should leave the town, only making the condition that but thirty wagons should cross the Neck at a time. A great many availed themselves of the permission; so many, that the Tories were alarmed, and they alarmed the general. On the day of the battle, two hundred Tories had offered him their services, and were enrolled under Ruggles of Hardwick, who, it is said, was the best soldier in the colonies. Old people used to say he should have been the commander-in-chief of the American army, had he not been on the wrong side. The Tories thought the presence of the inhabitants necessary to save the town; that the American army would burn it. At last they threatened to lay down their arms, and leave the town themselves, if Gage permitted farther departure of the inhabitants; and Gage gave way.

Meanwhile the Provincial Congress had prepared the statement of the battle of Lexington, which we described in the last chapter Warren gave the following order to Capt. John Derby : —

In Committee of Safety, April 27, 1775.

Resolved, That Capt. Derby be directed, and he hereby is directed, to make for Dublin, or any other good port in Ireland, and from thence to cross to Scotland or England, and hasten to London. This direction is given, that, so he may escape all cruisers that may be in the chops of the channel to stop the communication of the provincial intelligence to the agent. He will forthwith deliver his papers to the agent on reaching London.

J. Warren, Chairman.
P.S. — You are to keep this order a profound secret from every person on earth.

(cont'd page 66)

***

Portrait of Joseph Warren, President, Massachusetts Provincial Congress. Oil on canvas by Gregory Lawler © 2017 Collection of Shane Newell. Photograph© Newell 2017

The Letters of Joseph Warren

May 3, 1775

"With the greatest deference, we beg leave to suggest that a powerful army on the side of America hath been considered by this Congress as the only means left to stem the rapid progress of tyrannical ministry...

Without force superior to our enemies, we must reasonably expect to become the victims of their relentless fury; With such a force, we may still have hopes of seeing an immediate end put to the unhuman ravages of mercenary troops in America, and the wicked authors of our miseries, brought to condign punishment by the indignation of our brethren in Great Britain."

Joseph Warren, President Massachusetts Provincial Congress at Watertown

***

"Not Fifty People In The Whole Colony Ever Expected Any Blood Would Be Shed"

***

Cambridge, May 15, 1775.

"Dear Sir, – I received your very kind letter, enclosing a bill of exchange of four hundred and twenty dollars, in favor of the distressed poor of Boston, upon Mr. Rotch, which I shall take the first opportunity of sending to him, not doubting but it will be duly honored. The sympathy which you discover to have, both in our sufferings and successes in opposing the enemies to the country, is a fresh proof of that benevolence and public spirit which I ever found in you. I rejoice that our friends in Philadelphia are united, and that all are at last brought to see the barbarous scheme of oppression which Administration has formed.

We are all embarked in one bottom: if one colony is enslaved, she will be immediately improved as an engine to subdue the others. This our enemies know, and for this cause they have used, every art to divide us one from the other, to encourage every groundless prejudice, which they could hope to separate us. Our arch-traitor, Hutchinson, has labored hard in this service.

He seems to have fully adopted old Juno's maxim, – "Flectere si nequeo superos, Acheronta movebo."

I send you a few extracts from some of his letters, which have fortunately fallen in my hands. I likewise send you a pamphlet containing the regulations for the army. You are kind enough to say, that our friends in Philadelphia will assist with whatever they can, when they know our wants, which fills us with a lively sense of the generosity of your colony. To say the truth, we are in want of almost every thing, but of nothing so much as arms and ammunition; for, although much time has been spent in procuring these articles, yet the people never seemed in earnest about the matter until after the engagement of the 19th ult.: and I verily believe, that the night preceding the barbarous outrages committed by the soldiery at Lexington, Concord, &c., there were not fifty people in the whole colony that ever expected any blood would be shed in the contest between us and Great Britain.

The repeated intelligence I received from the best authority, of the sanguinary, malicious temper of the present Administration, together with a perfect knowledge of the inhumanity and wickedness of the villains at Boston who had the ear of General Gage, compelled me to believe that matters would be urged to the last extremity.

I am, dear sir, with much regard and esteem, your most humble servant,

Joseph Warren
To Joseph Reed, Esq.
Philadelphia
PS The Extracts of Mr. Hutchinsons Letters which promised you & I had not time to take off, but have sent a Number to Mr. Sam Adams who will gladly communicate them to you if you think them worth your perusal.—
Cambridge, May 15, 1775

***

To the Honorable Congress for the Colony of New York
Gentlemen
Your noble Exertions in the common Cause, your Zeal for the Maintenance of the Rights of America & the Sympathizing Concern, with which we know you look on our suffering, encourages us to represent to you the distressed State of this Colony.

Our Capital is filled with disciplined troops, thoroughly equipped with every thing necessary to render them formidable. A train of Artillery as complete as can be conceived of, a full supply of Arms and Ammunition, and an absolute command of the Harbor of Boston, which puts it in their Power to furnish themselves with whatever they shall think convenient by Sea, are such Advantages as must render our Contest with them in every view extremely difficult.

We suffer at present the greatest Inconveniences from a want of a sufficient Quantity of Powder, without this every attempt to defend ourselves or annoy our Enemies must prove abortive; We have taken every step to avail ourselves of this Article, by drawing into our General Magazine whatever could be spared from the Respective Towns of this Colony; But the frequent Skirmishes we have had, has greatly diminished our Stock, and we are now under the most alarming Apprehensions; that notwithstanding the Bravery of our Troops, (whom we think we can without boasting declare are ready to encounter every Danger for the preservation of the Rights & Liberties of America) we shall barely for the want of the Means of Defense fall at last a prey to our enemies. We therefore most earnestly beseech you that you would if possible afford in some Relief in this Respect, by lending or selling to us some part of the Powder in your Colony, we readily conceive the Unwillingness with which you must part with so necessary an Article at this Time, we know you have not the Quantity you would wish to keep for your own use, we apply to you, not because we suppose you have a Surplussage, but because we are in the most distressing Want. We beg therefore that we may be not be suffered to perish, we have taken such Steps as we have great Reason to hope will in a short Time furnish us sufficiently with Powder, and if we can be assisted until that arrives, we doubt not but that we shall be able to baffle the designs of our Enemies, and be greatly instrumental in preserving the Rights and Liberties of all America. We must request that whatever aid you shall find it in your Power to give us may be in the most secret Manner, as a knowledge of our Deficiency in the Article of Powder, before we are supplied might be attended with the most fatal consequences.

We are Gentlemen with Great Respect

Your Affectionate Brethren of very Humble Servants,
Artemas Ward General of the Massachusetts Army
Jos Warren Chairman of the Committee of Safety,
Moses Gill Chairman of the Committee of Supplies

P.S. We beg what Powder you can possibly spare may be immediately conveyed to us by Land in the way least liable to be suspected by any Persons who may correspond with the Enemy.

Cambridge 4 June 1775

How the War Began: The Siege at Boston (cont'd)

Freighted with his precious cargo of depositions, Capt. Derby cracked on, and outsailed everything on the seas. "The Sukey," Capt. Brown, had sailed four days before him, with Gage's account; but Derby arrived in London eleven days in advance of her. Here is Horace Walpole's account of the reception of the news, in a letter to Horace Mann: —

June 5, 1775.

You must lower your royal crest a little, for your Majesty's forces have received a check in America; but this is too sad a subject for mirth. I cannot tell you anything very positively: the ministers, nay, the orthodox Gazette, holds its tongue. This day se'nnight, it was divulged by a "London Evening Post" extraordinary, that a ship on its way to Lisbon happened to call at England, and left some very wonderful accounts, nay, and affidavits, saying, to wit, that Gen. Gage had sent nine hundred men to nail up the cannon, and seize a magazine at Concord, of which the accidental captain owns, two cannon were spiked or damaged. A hundred and fifty Americans, who swear they were fired on first, disliked the proceeding, returned blows, and drove back the party. Lord Percy was dispatched to support them; but, new recruits arriving, his Lordship sent for better advice, which he received, and it was to retire, which he did. The king's troops lost a hundred and fifty, the enemy not a hundred. The captain was sent for to be examined, but refused. He says Gage sent away a sloop four days before he sailed, which sloop, I suppose, is gone to Lisbon; for in eight days we have no news of it. The public were desired by authority to suspend their belief; but their patience is out; and they agree in believing the first account, which seems the rather probable, in that another account is come of the mob having risen in New York, between anger and triumph — have seized, unloaded, and destroyed the cargoes of two ships that were going with supplies to Gage; and, by all accounts, that whole continent is in a flame. So here is the fatal war commenced.

"The child that is unborn shall rue The hunting of that day."

This allusion to Lisbon may have been a mask. Derby does not seem to have gone to Lisbon. If he did, he was back at Salem on the 18th of

July; and here is the account then published of his mission: —

[Extract of a letter from London, dated June 1, 1775.]

"*The intelligence, by Capt. D., of the defeat of G. Gage's men under Lord P. by the Americans, of the 19th of April last, has given very general pleasure here, as the newspapers will testify. 'Tis not with certainty that one can speak of the disposition of people in England; with respect to the contest with America, though Ave are clear that the friends of America increase every day, particularly since the above intelligence. It Ls believed the ministers have not as yet formed any plans in consequence of the action of April 19th. They are in total confusion and consternation, and wait for G. Gage's dispatches by the, Capt. Brown.*

In the same paper with the above, in the news from London, appears the following: —

London, May 31.
Lord North, when he received the unhappy news to government, that the provincials had defeated Gen. Gage's troops, was struck with *astonishment, turned pale, and did not utter a syllable for some minutes.*

The captain of the vessel who lately brought the news of the defeat of the king's forces has been sent for by the Privy Council; but he is too honest a man to dissemble his sentiments, or conceal the truth.

***

Nothing was ever more successful than the enterprise by which the American account of the opening of the war was thus given to all Europe in advance of the English general's: indeed, it reminds one of the skill with which our Southern brothers kept a news-maker squat by the side of each telegraph-office of importance in England, through the late war; only, in the case of Lexington, the Provincial Congress took depositions, and sent the truth. The ministry, as Walpole says, begged people to suspend their judgment; that the news was probably false. On which Arthur Lee published a card today that all the papers were at the Mansion House, and any man might see them there.

Walpole's allusion to "Chevy-Chase" is suggestive. It had been made on this side,. and so made, that the Percy of that day understood it.

As his brigade marched through Roxbury on the fatal 19th of April, the band was playing, by way of contempt, "Yankee Doodle." A smart boy observing it, as the troops passed through Roxbury, made himself extremely merry with the circumstance, jumping and laughing, so as to attract the notice of his lordship, who asked him at what he was laughing so heartily, and was answered, " To think how you will dance by and by to Chevy- Chase.'" Gordon adds, that the repartee stuck by his lordship the whole day; and Gordon, for an anecdote like this, is first-rate authority.

Meanwhile, as a part of the understanding by which the poor of Boston were permitted to come out, the Tories outside were permitted to come in. Here is Lady Frankland's request for a pass, and the inventory of a baronet's wife proposing to emigrate. She addresses it to Dr. Warren : —

Hopkiton, May 15, 1775.
Lady Frankland presents her compliments to the Committee of Safety; begs leave to acquaint them, that, according to their request, she has sent in a list of things necessary for her intended voyage; which, obtained. Lady F. -will esteem a peculiar favor, and begs she may

have her pass for Thursday.

A list of things for Lady Frankland: Six trunks, one chest, three beds and bedding, six wethers [a castrated ram], two pigs, one small keg of pickled tongues, some hay, three bags of corn.

The Congress granted the prayer, with the courtesy and precision of one of Homer's heroes.

Resolved, that Lady Frankland be permitted to go to Boston with the following articles, viz.: seven trunks; all the beds with the furniture to them; all the boxes and crates; a basket of chickens, and a bag of corn; two barrels and a hamper ; two horses and two chaises, and all the articles in the chaise, excepting arms and ammunition ; one phæton, some tongues, ham, and veal, and sundry small bundles.

Lady Frankland is the charming woman whom Dr. Holmes has immortalized; who saved her husband's life when Lisbon fell in ruins. She was now leaving, for the last time, the stately mansion in Hopkinton, which is described in Mrs. Stowe's "Oldtown*."

The estimate made at the Provincial headquarters was that five thousand of the people of Boston would be destitute when they came out; and the Congress assigned them homes in every town in the colony. But no such number as five thousand came out, and Whigs and Tories suffered the hardships of the siege together.

In the month of May, during the siege, we have no local newspaper. "The Boston Evening Post " was the last which kept its flag flying. In its weekly issue of the 24th of April appear these sad little announcements: —
Boston, April 24, 1775.

The unhappy transactions of last week are so variously related that we shall not at present undertake to give any particular account thereof.

The Printers of the Boston Evening Post hereby inform the Town, that they shall desist publishing their Papers after this Day, till Matters are in a more settled State.

***

On the 25th of May, Gens. Howe, Clinton, and Burgoyne, arrived with re-enforcements. So confident were they of what our Yankees call " a good time," that it is on record that they had provided themselves with hooks, lines, and other fishing-tackle, for their amusement. Alas! unless they bobbed for flounders and tomcod from Long Wharf, they had little chance that way.

When they were going into Boston, they met a packet coming out, bound to Newport, when Burgoyne asked the skipper of the packet, "What news is there?" And being told that Boston was surrounded by ten thousand country people, asked, "How many regulars are there in Boston?" And being answered, "About five thousand," cried out with astonishment, "What, ten thousand peasants keep five thousand king's troops shut up! Well, let us get in, and we'll soon find elbow-room." Hence this phrase, "elbow-room," was much used through all the Revolution. Gen. Burgoyne is designated by " Elbow-room " in the satires of the time. It is said that he loved a joke, and used to relate, that after his Canada reverses, while a prisoner of war, he was received with great courtesy by the Boston people as he stepped from the Charlestown ferry-boat ; but he was really annoyed, when an old lady, perched on a shed above the crowd, cried out at the top of a shrill voice, " Make way, make way ! The general's coming! Give him elbow-room!"

The British works in Boston were considerably enlarged as the month went by. A report by Col. Heath, which is preserved in his MSS., and has never, until now, been printed, gives the following estimate of Gage's forces, and a statement, which will be interesting to Boston people, of the fortifications in the month of March : —

"The [British] army at present consists of about 2,850 men, encamped as follows : —

On Boston Common, about;...... 1,700
On Fort Hill, about...... 400
On Boston Neck, about.....340
In the Barracks at Castle William 330
Quartered in King Street......80
Total 2,850

"*Two mudd Breastworks have been erected by them on Boston Neck, at the distance of about ninety or one hundred rods in front of the old fortifications; the works well constructed and well executed; the thickness of the merlons or parapet, about nine feet; the height, about eight feet; the width of the ditch at the top, about twelve feet, at the bottom five feet; the depth, ten feet. These works are nearly completed, and at present mounted with ten brass and two Iron Cannon: a Barrack is erecting behind the Breastwork, on the north side of the Neck. The old Fortification, at the entrance of the Town of Boston [where Dover Street now crosses], is repairing and greatly strengthened, by the addition of timber and earth to the walls, of about twelve feet: those works are in considerable forwardness; and at present ten pieces of Iron Cannon are mounted on the old platforms. A Block house, brought from Governor's Island, is erecting on the south side of the Neck, at the distance of about forty or fifty rods from the old fortification: this work is but just begun."*

***

The month of May did not pass without frequent alarms, some well and some ill-founded. On the 8th of May, there was a rumor of another "excursion," so well defined, that the minute-men and militia of the ten next towns were called into service. On the 13th, Putnam marched twenty-two hundred men into Charlestown, quite to the ferry, and back to Cambridge. They were unmolested by Gage, or by his ships, though they passed within range. On the 21st, all Weymouth, Braintree, and Hingham, turned out to defend Grape Island. Warren was under fire through the whole of this affair; and his modest account of it is the best we have. On the 27th, the chief skirmish of all these took place at Hog Island, next Noddle's Island, which is now East Boston. In this "engagement," the English general lost a sloop, twelve swivels, and several men. Gen. Putnam was in command on our side; and an exaggerated report of the affair helped to make him a major-general. On the whole, in these matters of the islands, the besiegers did better than the besieged. Gen. Gage hardly understood yet, perhaps, how soon he should need fresh provisions. In two different affairs, the provincials took off thirteen hundred sheep from under his eyes. The Provincial Congress were more thoughtful, when they refused to let Lady Frankland bring in her "wethers."

It was on the 10th of May that Ethan Allen took Ticonderoga; telling the sleepy colonel in command, "that he took it in the name of the Great Jehovah and the Continental Congress. The careful annalists observe that the congress did not meet till after the surrender. Little did Allen care. His dispatch to the Massachusetts Provincial Congress makes no mention of Arnold, who had associated himself with the expedition.

Part Six
The Battle on Bunkers Hill[1]

Centennial Publication: *One Hundred Years Ago: How the War Began* by Edward Hale

George Bunker, an English Puritan, had left England, and arrived in Charlestown in New England, as early as 1634. In the next year he was made a freeman. New England antiquaries will know what is meant, when we say that he was disarmed in November, 1637, as a supporter of Wheelwright: but in the following year he was made the constable of Charlestown; and in 1639 the General Court made to him a grant of fifty acres. He was among the last "batch" of people to whom fifty acres was granted, on the plea that the "first planters" were allowed fifty acres to each person.

Whether he took these special fifty acres on and around the hill which still bears his name, I cannot tell. But he is the man who owned this hill; and, because he owned it, it was and is "Bunker's Hill." He lived and died, unconscious that Bunker's Hill was to be one of the important places in history, and a point where one of the decisive battles of the world was to be fought.

Bunker's Hill, the highest emimence in the peninsula of Charlestown, is so high, that it "commands," as military men say, the northern part of Boston, and especially the northern part of the

---

1. It was later determined that the battle mainly took place on Breed's Hill but by that time, the name Bunker had been permanently associated with the battle.

harbor of Boston. On the south-east of Boston, the hills of what we call South Boston, which were called "Dorchester Heights" a hundred years ago, command the southern part of Boston, and the whole of Boston harbor. The evident military value of the Charlestown and Dorchester Heights was perceived at once by both parties, as soon as the "siege of Boston" began.

The Committee of Safety, as the reader must remember, took the place, in the extemporized government of Massachusetts, of the governor. The Committee of Safety was the Executive [Joseph Warren as Chairman]. Here is' their order for the occupation of the hill, —

"Whereas, it appears of importance to the safety of this colony that possession of the hill called Bunker's Hill, in Charlestown, be securely kept and defended, and also, some one hill or hills on Dorchester Neck be likewise secured: therefore, Resolved unanimously. That it be recommended to the council of war, that the above-mentioned Bunker's Hill be maintained by sufficient forces being posted there; and, as the peculiar situation of Dorchester Neck is unknown to this committee, they desire that the council of war take and pursue such steps respecting the same as to them shall appear to be for the security of this colony."

Engraving, front inside cover of *Stories about General Warren in Relation to the Fifth of March Massacre and the Battle of Bunker Hill*. This small and rare book was published in 1835 by James Loring of Boston. The author is listed as "A Lady of Boston" and later discovered to be Rebecca Warren Brown. Rebecca Warren was daughter of Dr. John Warren, and the niece of Dr. Joseph Warren. The engraving has little likeness to Joseph Warren and hopefully less likeness to his dear mother. The caption under the engraving serves as a literary precursor to the noble words of Tom Joad in John Steinbeck's *The Grapes of Wrath* (1939) regarding the fight for freedom. It reads *"When Gen. Warren's mother first saw him after the escape from the Battle of Lexington, she entreated him, with tears in her eyes, not again to risk a life so dear to her, and so necessary to his country. "Wherever danger is, dear mother"* was his reply, *"there your son be, now is no time for one of America's children to shrink from the most hazardous duty. I will either see my country free, or shed my last drop of blood to make her so..."*

The Battle on Bunkers Hill 73

Another engraving of Joseph Warren leaving for the Battle of Bunker Hill. This hand-colored engraving is entitled "Gen. Warren taking leave of his wife and child on the eve of the battle of Bunker Hill." Engraved by Thomas Kelly (1795-1841) for Columbian Magazine, Boston circa 1825. Joseph Warren's wife, Elizabeth Hooten, died in 1773. The Battle of Bunker Hill took place in 1775. The only woman Warren could have been leaving at home, besides his dear mother as shown in the previous Plate, is Mercy Scollay, to whom Joseph had recently engaged to wed. Warren had four children with Elizabeth. Mercy helped raise the children after Elizabeth's passing and subsequently helped provide guardianship after Joseph's death. The image helped preserve Warren's legacy into the nineteenth century. Any truer an image of his leaving his fiancé and four children as orphans would be more heart-breaking than the imaginary scene.

Under this order of the committee. Gen. Ward directed a detachment under Col. Prescott, — consisting of Prescott's, Frye's, and Bridge's regiments, — and a fatigue-party of two hundred Connecticut troops, to parade at six o'clock in the evening, with all the intrenching-tools, in the Cambridge camp. They were also ordered to furnish themselves with packs and blankets, and with provisions for twenty- four hours. Also Capt. Samuel Gridley's company of artillery, of forty-nine men and two field-pieces, was ordered to parade. The Connecticut men, drafted from several companies, were put under the gallant Thomas Knowlton, a captain in Gen. Putnam's regiment.

Militia on way to the Battle at Bunker Hill. Supplement to the Boston Globe 1910. Collection of Shane Newell.

They all marched from Cambridge at nine o'clock, and arrived in an hour at the top of Banker's Hill, which is indeed but just inside of Charlestown Neck. From the top of Bunker's Hill, to Copp's Hill in Boston, where, the English had a battery, is almost exactly one mile as the bird flies; to the top of Beacon Hill, as it then existed, was a little less than a mile and a half. Beacon Hill was then one hundred' and thirty-eight feet above the sea ; Bunker's Hill was one hundred and ten feet above the sea ; and Copp's Hill, about fifty-eight feet. If the purpose of fortifying Bunker's Hill were to attack the fleet in the harbor, that purpose would hardly be attained by a post there. To a certain extent, the vessels could be sheltered from Bunker's Hill by Breed's Hill, as it has since been called, a lower eminence, sixty-two feet above the sea, directly in line from Bunker's Hill to the Copp's Hill batteries.

Again: if the object were simply to keep the English troops from seizing the heights, it was necessary to take possession of both summits, the higher and the lower, at the same time. In saying this, I speak on very high military authority. Had the entrenching party satisfied themselves with entrenching on Bunker's Hill only, the English commanders would have immediately formed under the cover of Breed's Hill, and could even have fortified themselves on the southern slope of that hill, in works that could not have been reached from batteries on Bunker's Hill. The exact curve fire of our times, which drops shell with precision on the heads of troops unprotected by bomb-proof, was not one of the accomplishments of these days, nor was it possible to the artillery in possession of the rebels.

***

"Bunker Hill 1775" by American folk artist Brian Scully. The folk aft "tavern door" quadriptych (four panel aft) squares off Major General Joseph Warren with General William Howe and the burning of Charles Town with a bayonet attack on British soldiers. Private Collection.

Major General Joseph Warren in rare hand-colored engraving from the original picture by Chappel, in possession of the Publishers Johnsons, Fry & Co Publishers, New York.

Gridley, the colonel of engineers, insisted that some decision should be made; and when, after more than an hour, it was determined to begin on the lower hill, he marked out his lines skillfully. At midnight, six hundred men were at work heartily but silently on the redoubt which he laid out. It seems to have been skillfully planned. It was eight rods long on its strongest and longest point, which faced Charlestown. The two sides were nearly as long. The eastern side, towards Boston, commanded an extensive field, where, as on the south side, the ground descended steeply. The north side, towards Bunker's Hill, was left more open. A breastwork extended about one hundred yards towards the north, following the slight decline of the hill on that side. This work ended at or near a slough, or swampy place, on the north side of the hill. Such was the work planned by Gridley, well forwarded before daylight, and advanced by the steady labor of the force employed till nearly eleven o'clock. At Putnam's request, the entrenching-tools were then sent back to him at Bunker's Hill, where he was eager to establish a strong enough work to hold that hill also. In a military point of view, as has been said, Putnam was undoubtedly right in his determination to do so.

"Warren tendering his services to General Putnam just before the Battle of Bunker Hill."
Supplement to Frank Leslie's Illustrated Newspaper 1875. Engraving.

At four o'clock in the morning, "The Lively," Capt. Linzee, an English vessel which lay in the river, off the present Navy Yard, opened fire on the works. The sound broke the silence of the morning, and called the people of the North End to see the scene. It was thus the place of Linzee to fire the first shot upon Prescott's works. Two generations after, Prescott's grandson, the historian, William Hickling Prescott, married Linzee's grand-daughter. The swords which the two officers wore on the day of battle thus came into his peaceful possession. While he lived, they were crossed in his library; and after his death they were placed together in the Massachusetts Historical Library, in token and omen of the friendship between the two nations, which was to be sealed and made certain by the sacrifices of that day and of the war.

It is not so much the intention of this series of papers to go into every detail of those eventful days, as it is to show the reader in the nineteenth century how they were regarded in their time, and how he is best to arrange the various anecdotes which the anniversary celebrations are certain to call forward.

So soon as the artillery-fire of "The Lively," and Gridley's fire in reply, from his field-pieces, showed to Gage and the other English generals what was passing, they determined to attack the works before they were strengthened. Of their accounts, Burgoyne's is the most picturesque. It is in these words, in a letter to Lord Stanley, which was published as soon as it arrived in England: —

"On the 17th, at dawn of day, we found the enemy had pushed intrenchments with great diligence during the night, on the heights of Charlestown; and we evidently saw that every hour gave them fresh strength: it therefore became necessary to alter our plan, and attack on that side. Howe, as second in command, was detached with about two thousand men, and landed on the opposite side of this peninsula, covered with shipping, without opposition; he was to advance from thence up the hill which was over Charlestown, where the strength of the enemy lay : he had under him Brig. -Gen. Pigot. Clinton and myself took our stand (for we had not any fixed post) in a large battery directly opposite to Charlestown, which commanded it, and also scaled the heights above it, and thereby facilitating Howe's attack. Howe's disposition was exceedingly soldier-like: in my opinion it was perfect. As his first arm advanced up the hill, they met with a thousand impediments from, strong forces, and were much exposed. They were also exceedingly hurt by musketry from Charlestown, though Clinton and I did not perceive it until Howe sent His word by a boat, and desired us to set fire to the town, which was immediately done. We threw a parcel of shells, and the whole was instantly in flames. Our battery afterwards kept an incessant fire on the heights. It was seconded by a number of frigates, floating-batteries, and our ship-of-the-line. ...

-A moment of the day was critical. Howe's left were staggered: two battalions had been sent to re-enforce them; but we perceived them on the beach, seeming in embarrassment what way to march. Clinton then, next for business, took the part, without waiting for orders, to throw himself into a boat to head them: he arrived in time to be of service. The day ended with glory, and the success was most important, considering the ascendency it gave the regular troops ; but the loss was uncommon in officers for the numbers engaged."

Compare this account with that made by order of the Provincial Committee of Safety. This was prepared by Rev. Dr. Cooper, Rev., Mr. Gardner, and Rev. Peter Thacher; the skill of the ministers as men of literature being called upon, drolly enough, for a report, which was intended as a correction of Gage's statements. It is understood that the report was drawn up by Thacher, who saw the battle from the other side of Mystic River. Their narrative of the action itself is in these words: —

"*Between twelve and one o'clock, a number of boats and barges, filled with the regular troops from Boston, were observed approaching towards Charlestown: these troops landed at a place called 'Moreton's Point,' situated a little to the eastward of our works. This brigade formed upon their landing, and stood thus formed till a second detachment arrived from Boston to join them: having sent out large flank guards, they began a very slow march towards our lines. At this instant, smoke and flames were seen to arise from the town of Charlestown, which had been set on fire by the enemy, that the smoke might cover their attack upon our lines, and, perhaps, with a design to rout or destroy one or two regiments of provincials who had been posted in that town. If either of these was their design, they were disappointed; for the wind, shifting on a sudden, carried the smoke another way; and the regiments were already removed.*

The provincials, within their intrenchments, impatiently waited the attack of the enemy, and reserved their fire till they came within ten or twelve rods; and then began a furious discharge of small-arms. This fire arrested the enemy, which they for some time returned without advancing a step, and then retreated, in disorder and with, great precipitation, to the place of landing; and some of them sought refuge even within their boats. Here the officers were observed, by the spectators on the opposite shore, to run down to them, using the most passionate gestures, and pushing the men forward with their swords. At length they were rallied, and marched up, with apparent reluctance, towards the intrenchment. The Americans again reserved their fire until the enemy came within five or six rods, and a second time put the regulars to flight, who ran in great confusion towards their boats.

Similar and superior exertions were now necessarily made by the officers, which, notwithstanding the men discovered an almost insuperable reluctance to fighting in this cause, were again successful. They formed once more; and, having brought some cannon to bear in such a manner as to rake the inside of the breastwork from one end of it to the other, the provincials retreated within their little fort. The ministerial army now made a decisive effort. The fire from the ships and batteries, as well as from the cannon in front of their army, was redoubled. The officers in the rear of the army were observed to goad forward the men with renewed exertions; and they attacked the redoubt on three sides at once. The breastwork on the outside of the fort was abandoned; the ammunition of the provincials was expended; and few of their arms were fixed with bayonets. Can it, then, be wondered that the word was given by the commander of the party to retreat? But this he delayed till the redoubt was half filled with regulars, and the provincials had kept the enemy at bay some time, confronting them with the butt-ends of their muskets. The retreat of this little handful of brave men would have been effectually cut off, had it not happened that the flanking party of the enemy, which was to have come upon the

The Battle on Bunkers Hill

"Warren the Warrior" by Historical Artist Dan Nance, measuring 28.5" X 22.5" acrylic/oil on canvas. This painting depicts Warren moments before British troops made a third advance that would break the American lines. British Troops had been repelled twice earlier in the day. In the third advance, the American line runs out of gunpowder. For months Warren had pled with the adjacent Colonies to send gunpowder, but supplies were too short to spare. As the militia begins to retreat, Warren draws his sword beneath the fateful grey skies. *Collection of Shane Newell.*

Joseph Warren had privately studied military strategy and he had served bravely in battles at Lexington, Concord, Grape Island, Noddle's Island, and Bunker Hill. Warren's willingness to set aside the pen and pick up a sword was far more warrior-like than his political contemporaries. Warren dispatched Paul Revere to warn Sam Adams and John Hancock that the British were marching for Lexington and Concord. They both left town without delay. As President of the Provincial Congress, Joseph Warren was the only political figure who remained to defend the Providence against her enemy. Warren's presence on the battlefield gave moral support to the militia and to the cause of their service. Warren was the highest ranking political leader and military officer during the military successes in Boston in the Spring of 1775—a feat that would not be eclipsed for another eighteen months when General George Washington would lead the Battle of Trenton during the American Revolution. Save perhaps, the retreat of the British Army from Boston under the threat of cannon artillery commandeered from Fort Ticonderoga and carried to American forces at Dorchester Heights – a plan initially conceived by Joseph Warren and John Brown.

The Battle on Bunkers Hill

back of the redoubt, was checked by a party of the provincials, who fought with the utmost bravery, and kept them from advancing farther than the beach. The engagement of these two parties was kept up with the utmost vigor; and it must be acknowledged that this party of the ministerial troops evidenced a courage worthy a better cause. All their efforts, however, were insufficient to compel the provincials to retreat till their main body had left the hill. Perceiving this was done, they then gave ground, but with more regularity than could be expected of troops who had no longer been under discipline, and many of whom had never before seen an engagement."

The reader who did not know that these two narratives were, one by Gov. Burgoyne, who saw the action from Copp's Hill in Boston, and the other by Peter Thacher the minister who saw it from exactly the opposite side of the field, and with exactly opposite prejudices, would never know that the same action was described. It has been the business of every historian of the battle to collect the detail which shall fill up the narrative. This is to a great extent done; and, in the full detail given by Mr. Frothingham, The successive stages of the battle may be wrought out intelligibly.

The traditional three attacks unquestionably took place, although neither Burgoyne nor Gage alludes to them. The closing words of Peter Thacher's account allude to a feature in the action not so generally understood, — the almost independent position of the American left wing.

While Gen. Pigot with the English left was assailing the redoubt in the first of the three attacks. Gen. Howe led his right wing along the shore of Mystic River, hoping to turn the American lines. To prevent this, Col. Prescott had sent two field-pieces with Col. Knowlton and the Connecticut troops down the hill to the river. Knowlton was the officer on whom Washington passed so noble a eulogium the next year, when he was killed. He was killed in the region now comprised in the Central Park of New York; and Connecticut must see to it, that

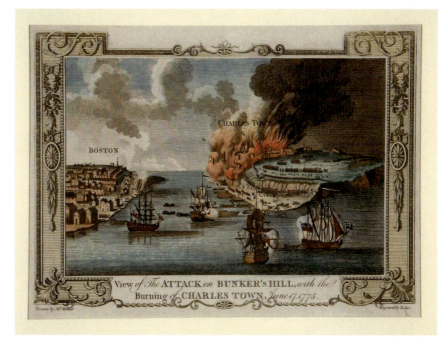

View of the attack on Bunker's Hill, with the burning of Charles Town, June 17, 1775. Drawn by Mr. Millar; engraved by Lodge, 1796. This drawing depicts the assault on Bunker Hill as four British warships landing troops and firing on Charlestown. A British battery on Copp's Hill in Boston also fires on Charlestown which is in flames. Library of Congress Prints and Photographs Division Washington, D.C. 20540 USA http://hdl.loc.gov/loc.pnp/pp.print

his monument is added to that of other heroes there. Knowlton had stationed himself near the southern front of Bunker's Hill proper, behind a fence, which was stone below, with two rails of wood above. He strengthened this line by a parallel line of fence, filling in between with grass. While he was thus engaged, he was re-enforced by Stark.

Stark's report is wretchedly meagre: —

"*Upon which I was required by the general to send a party, consisting of two hundred men, with officers, to their assistance; which order I readily obeyed, and appointed and sent Col. Wyman commander of the same. And about two o'clock in the afternoon express orders came for the whole of my regiment to proceed to Charlestown to oppose the enemy, who were landing on Charlestown Point. Accordingly we proceeded; and the battle soon came on, in which a number of officers belonging to my regiment were killed, and many privates killed and wounded.*"

From other accounts, we have more detail of the action here. Callender's American field-pieces opened on Howe's party with great effect. Knowlton bade his men hold their fire till the enemy came within fifteen rods, and they did so. When the word was given, the result was horrible to see or to tell. The companies were terribly cut up, wavered, broke, and retreated, as, at nearly the same time, Pigot's did before the redoubt, on the other wing of Howe's advance.

In the second attack on the redoubt, Howe directed his artillery to be served with grape. They had no proper balls, an incident frequently referred to. The artillery moved nearly up to the line of the breastwork in a narrow road, which will be seen upon the map, parallel with the Mystic, on the northern slope of Breed's Hill. The object was to rake the redoubt, and thus open a way for the infantry. A second time, Howe was in front of Stark and Knowlton. Both there and at the redoubt, the American fire was held as before, even to a shorter range. At both points the English gave way. This was the period when the English were re-enforced from Boston, and when Clinton joined them as related by Burgoyne.

***

In the third attack, the English artillery gained its position, so that it could enfilade the breastwork. The defenders of the breastwork took refuge in the redoubt. Prescott did not waver. Most of his men had but one round of ammunition, and few had more than three; but he bade them hold their fire as before, and they did till their enemy was within twenty yards. The English were now advancing in column, having been taught their terrible lesson by the former experiences.

The column wavered under Prescott's fire, but rushed on with the bayonet; and Clinton's and Pigot's men, on the southern and eastern sides, reached the shelter of its walls. Prescott bade the men who had no bayonets retire to the rear of the redoubt, and fire on the enemy as they mounted. A fine fellow climbed the southern side, cried, "The day is ours!" and fell. The whole front rank shared his fate. But the game was played. These were the last shots. The Englishmen poured over the parapet; and Prescott gave his unwilling order to retreat.

He always said, that, even without powder (and he had none), he could have held the hill, had his men had bayonets. The following very curious letter, is, I believe, the first allusion to the engagement, in the records of the Provincial Congress, after it occurred: — *Cambridge, June* 19, 1775.

It is requested that the troops may be supplied also with a large number of spears or lances for defending the breastworks. In the late action, spears Bought have saved the intrenchment. By order of the general.

Joseph Ward, Secretary.

84 The Battle on Bunkers Hill

Battle of Bunker's Hill. From the original picture by Alanzo Chappel, in possession of the Publishers Johnsons, Fry & Co Publishers, New York.

The Battle on Bunkers Hill   85

"Newell Convers Wyeth, "Warren's Address," 1922, oil on canvas, Permanent Collection of The Hill School, Pottstown, PA

"Warren's Address" the poem, by Pierpoint, John, The National Reader: A Selection of Exercises in Reading and Speaking, Designed to Fill the Same Place in the Schools of the United States that is Held in Those of Great Britain: Hilliard, Gray, Little and Wilkins, Boston, 1827, p. 250.

Stand! the ground's your own, my braves!
Will ye give it up to slaves?
Will ye look for greener graves?
Hope ye mercy still?
What's the mercy despots feel?
Hear it in that battle-peal!
Read it on yon bristling steel.
Ask it,–ye who will.
Fear ye foes who kill for hire?
Will ye to your homes retire?
Look behind you!–they're a-fire!
And, before you, see
Who have done it!–From the vale
On they come!–And will ye quail?–
Leaden rain and iron hail
Let their welcome be!
In the God of battles trust!
Die we may,–and die we must;–
But, O, where can dust to dust
Be consigned so well,
As where Heaven its dews shall shed
On the martyred patriot's bed,
And the rocks shall raise their head,
Of his deeds to tell!

86 The Battle on Bunkers Hill

An order was actually given for the manufacture of two thousand of these spears.

The redoubt was flanked on both sides; but all parties were too close for the English to fire, even if their pieces were charged, which is not probable. Warren was killed here; Gridley was wounded; and the Americans lost more men than at any period of the battle.

✷✷✷

American artist Don Troiani's oil painting entitled "The Redoubt – The Battle of Bunker Hill". Troiani collects period uniforms and accessories to insure every element in his work is correctly depicted. In this sequel to his earlier work entitled "Bunker Hill", "The Redoubt" places Joseph Warren in the foreground right-center defending the earthen fort while others escape behind him. As it had been described by eyewitness accounts, Warren is wearing a fine silk waistcoat and blue frock. Holding his sword, Warren takes a gallant stand facing the advancing regiment. Moments later, Warren is shot in the head and dies instantly. The British Army loses more than 1,000 men, the Americans only 450. The death of Joseph Warren turns the hilltop defense into the American War of Independence. The original measures 27" x 18", oil on canvas, dated 2009. Private Collection. Image licensed by Bridgeman Images.

Meanwhile our friends at the rail-fence, the left wing of the Americans, held their own. When Prescott's disorganized command had passed them, they covered his retreat, and retired in good order.

Now was the moment which Putnam had foreseen, for which he had been trying to fortify the higher hill. Pomeroy of Northampton joined him in trying to rally the retreating forces there. But it was not possible. The whole body retired over the Neck, and met the re-enforcements which had been ordered too late to their relief. One piece of cannon at the Neck opened on the enemy, and covered the retreat.

The following report is the brief account which the Massachusetts Congress sent to the Congress in Philadelphia. It is their report of June 20 ; and this passage follows that which has been cited above: —

"*Accordingly, on Friday evening, the 16th inst., this was effected by about twelve hundred men. About daylight, on Saturday morning, their line of circumvallation, on a small hill south of Bunker's Hill, in Charlestown, was closed : at this time, 'The Lively,' man-of-war, began to fire upon them. A number of our enemy's ships, tenders, cutters, scows, or floating-batteries, soon came up, from all which the fire was general by twelve o'clock. About two, the enemy began to land at a point which leads out from Noddle's Island, and immediately marched up to our intrenchments, from which they were twice repulsed, but, in the third attack, forced them. Our forces which were in the lines, as well as those sent for their support, were greatly annoyed on every side by balls and bombs from Copp's Hill, the ships, scows, &c. At this time the buildings in Charlestown appeared in flames in almost every quarter, kindled by hot balls, and is since laid in ashes. Though this scene was almost horrible, and altogether new to most of our men, yet many stood and received wounds by swords and bayonets, before they quitted their lines. At five o'clock the enemy ere in full possession of all the posts within the isthmus.*

"*The number of killed and wounded on our side is not known, but supposed by some to be about sixty or seventy, and by some considerably above that number. Our most worthy friend and president, Dr. Warren, lately elected a major-general, is among them. This loss we feel most sensibly. . . . The loss of the enemy is doubtless great. By an anonymous letter from Boston, we are told that they exult much in having gained the ground, though their killed and wounded are owned about one thousand; but this account exceeds every other estimation.*"

Prescott reported at headquarters, indignant that he had not been better supported, and offered to retake the hills, if he might have fifteen hundred men; but Ward, who was at least prudent, declined.

June 20, 1775.

"*We think it an indispensable duty to inform you that re-enforcements from Ireland, both of horse and foot, being arrived (the numbers unknown), and having good intelligence that Gen. Gage was about to take possession of the advantageous posts in Charlestown and on Dorchester Heights, the Committee of Safety advised that our troops should prepossess them, if possible.*"

Gen Gage, on the other side, knew very well at what terrible cost his victory had been won. Here is his letter to Lord Dartmouth: —

Boston, June 25, 1775.

"*The success, of which I send your lordship an account by the present opportunity, was very necessary in our present situation; and I wish most sincerely that it had not cost us so dear. The number of killed and wounded is greater than our forces* can afford to lose. The officers who were obliged to exert themselves have suffered very much; and we have lost some extremely good officers. The trials we have had show the rebels are not the despicable rabble too many have supposed them to be; and I find it owing to a military spirit encouraged among them for a few years past, joined with an uncommon degree of zeal and enthusiasm, that they are otherwise."

In a letter from Gen. Burgoyne of the English army, to Lord Stanley, he says, —

Boston, June 25, 1775.

"It was absolutely necessary that we should make ourselves masters of these heights" [Bunker's Hill and Dorchester Heights], "and we proposed to begin with Dorchester.' Everything was accordingly disposed. My two colleagues and myself (who, by the by, have never differed in one jot of military sentiment) had, in concert with Gen. Gage, formed the plan. Howe was to land with the transports on the point;

Clinton, in the centre; and I was to cannonade from the causeway or the Neck; each to take advantage of circumstances. The operations must have been very easy. This was to have been executed on the 18th" [Sunday].

Information of the. English movements and councils was so carefully conveyed to the Provincial Congress, that they knew all this as well as Burgoyne did. Here is their report, as they made it on the 20th of June to the Congress at Philadelphia. It is a good illustration of that game of chess which is called war; and the reader will see, that, in this case, the rebels won the first move. They say, — Horace Walpole had written, July 6, before they had the news: —

"The general complexion is war. AH advices speak the Americans determined; and report says, the government here intend to pursue the same plan. I told you at first I thought you and I should not see the end of this breach; and, if we do not, I know not what posterity will see, — the ruin of both countries, at least of this. Can we support the loss of America, or a long war?

There is a black cloud nearer. The livery of London have begun a quarrel with the king, and have actually proclaimed war on his ministers, as you will see by the papers. I do not take panic; but, if any blow should happen from America, the mob of London is a formidable fœ on a sudden. A minister may be executed before he is impeached; and considering the number of American merchants in the city, and of those who have connections in America, riots may be raised: but I hate to prophesy. I have always augured ill of this quarrel, and washed my hands of it"

After the dispatches came, he wrote: —

"Aug. 3. — In spite of all my modesty, I cannot help thinking I have a little something of the prophet about me. At least, we have not conquered America yet. I did not send you immediate word of theˆ victory at Boston, because the success not only seemed very equivocal, but because the conquerors lost three to one more than the vanquished. The last do not pique themselves upon modern good breeding, but level only at the officers, of whom they have slain a vast number. We are a little disappointed, indeed, at their fighting at all, which was not in our calculation. We knew we could conquer America in Germany, and I doubt had better have gone tither now for that purpose, as it does not appear hitherto to be quite so feasible in America itself. However, we are determined to know the worst, and are sending away all the men and ammunition we can muster. The Congress, not asleep neither, *have appointed a generalissimo, Washington, allowed a very able officer, who distinguished himself in the last war."*

All accounts agree in describing the terrible dismay felt in Boston as the wounded were brought over from the field. A letter published by Mr. Drake says that the loyalists sent down their carriages, chaises, and even hand-barrows to bring them up from the boats; and old people remember hearing their mothers tell of blood dropping from the carts upon the pavement. Gen. Howe was said to have said, "They may talk of their Mindens and their Fontenoys; but there was no such fire there as here." In truth, the French at Minden lost seven thousand men out of fifty thousand.

Howe lost at Bunker's Hill one thousand and fifty-four men from a force which is variously stated as two thousand, three thousand, and four thousand. In the history of the Fifty-second Regiment, the statement is made, that one of their light companies, led by Howe himself against Stark and Knowlton, had every man either killed or wounded.

Howe escaped without hurt; but it is remembered that his white silk stockings were bloody from the blood which men had left on the long grass through which he had to lead his troops. He quite fulfilled the promise he made in the speech which he addressed to his own men before the assault, "I shall not desire one of you to go a step farther than I shall go myself at your head."

It should be remembered, that, from 1762 to 1775, the English army had not been under fire. To most of the privates, war was probably as new as to their enemy. This may account for the exposure of the officers. One hundred and fifty-seven officers were Id lied and wounded in a total loss of one thousand and fifty-four.

The loss of the Americans was one hundred and forty killed, two hundred and seventy-one wounded; and they lost thirty prisoners. Their force engaged was about fifteen hundred; but at Bunker's Hill the larger, and on the way there, they must have had, not under fire, a thousand more men.

90 The Battle on Bunkers Hill

 "Dulce et decorum est pro patria mori"
"It is sweet to die for the fatherland"
Said to be the final words of Joseph Warren
June 17, 1775

Designed for martyrdom rather than historical accuracy. Photograph© 2017 Museum of Fine Arts, Boston The Death of General Warren at the Battle of Bunker's Hill, 17 June, 1775, after 1815 – before 1831, by John Trumbull, American, 1756-1843, Oil on canvas, 50.16 x 75.56 cm (19 ¾ x 29 ¾ in.) Gift of Howland S. Warren. 1977.853

The Battle on Bunkers Hill

"THE DEATH OF WARREN after Copley. Drawn by John Norman. Engraved by Brackenridge. Published 1776. Print shows Joseph Warren on bended knee, right hand over chest, left hand on rifle for support, after being mortally wounded during the battle of Bunker Hill, three soldiers stand nearby. Caption and Image: Library of Congress Rare Book and Special Collections Division Washington, D.C. 20540 USA

"*Contemplez l'ouvrage de pouvoir arbitraire*" drawn by Jacques François. Engraved by Jean-Baptiste. Published 1782. Imaginary scene depicting the funeral of Joseph Warren. Library of Congress Rare Book and Special Collections Division Washington, D.C. 20540 USA

"My bursting Heart must find vent at my pen. I have just heard that our dear Friend Dr. Warren is no more but fell gloriously fighting for his Country — saying better to die honourably in the field than ignominiously hang upon the Gallows. Great is our Loss. He has distinguished himself in every engagement, by his courage and fortitude, by animating the Soldiers and leading them on by his own example."...

"I cannot compose myself to write further."[1]

"Looking at it my whole frame contracted, my blood shivered, and I felt a faintness at my heart.[2]"

1. Letter from Abigail Adams to John Adams, 18 - 20 June 1775 [electronic edition]. Adams Family Papers: An Electronic Archive. Massachusetts Historical Society. http://www.masshist.org/digitaladams/

2. Abigail Adams to Mrs. John Shaw, March 4, 1786, in Letters of Mrs. Adams, the Wife of John Adams, ed. Charles Francis Adams (Boston, 1840), 324, regarding her seeing John Trumbull's oil on canvas painting entitled "The Death of General Warren at the Battle of Bunker's Hill, 17 June, 1775."

Abigail Adams

Part Seven
Remembering Joseph Warren

Eliphalet Newell[1] was a Boston Tea Party participant, member of the Boston militia, Captain of the first Massachusetts regiment at the Battle of Bunker Hill, and artillery officer of the Revolutionary Army. On December 11, 1777, he became an initiated Freemason at St. Andrews' Lodge in Boston. He was a baker by trade and a Masonic brother of Dr. Joseph Warren. His Charlestown tavern, which still stands today, was built in 1780 and named in honor of his fallen friend. Its large sign, which swung from a high post, portrayed Warren in his Masonic insignia as Grand Master.[2] The sign, according to accounts, also depicted sprigs of Acadia which symbolize the immortality of the soul. Neither the original sign, nor anything remotely like it, hangs at the Warren Tavern today. The sign may have been the first

Reproduction of the original Warren Tavern Sign by Walker's Colonial American Sign Company of York, Pa. Collection of Shane Newell.

"monument" constructed in honor of Joseph Warren.

Adjacent to Newell's house was a large hall, which was later called Warren Hall. The selectmen held their meetings at his house; and it is said that, while they were in session, Newell would sit and smoke his long pipe in an adjoining room until what he considered to be a reasonable amount of time had elapsed, at which point he would make his entrance, and, regardless of the town business, his usual address would be, "Mr. Chairman, did you say punch or flip?" The prompt was Newell's way of suggesting it was time for either juice or alcohol. Flip is a warm frothy ale and rum beverage popular in colonial times.

1. Although I may be a descendant of the same Newell family as Eliphalet [Abraham Newell, b. 1555, England], I only mention this coincidence as an unexpected discovery several years into assembling this book. *Shane Newell.*

2. A Century of Town Like: A History of Charlestown, Massachusetts, 1775-1887 by James F. Hunnewell.

In 1794, King Solomon's Lodge of Freemason's erected a monument to the memory of Warren and his associates, who fell in the battle on Bunker Hill.

This monument stood outside of the redoubt, on the spot where Gen. Warren was supposed to have fallen. It was a handsome structure, composed of a very graceful Tuscan pillar, about twenty feet high, standing on a pedestal ten or twelve feet high, and surmounted by a golden urn, bearing the inscription, "J. W., aged 35,"[1] entwined with masonic emblems. The south side of the pedestal bore the following inscription: —

Erected A. D. 1794,
BY
King Solomon's Lodge
of
Freemasons,
(Constituted in Charlestown, 1783,)

IN MEMORY OF
MAJOR GENERAL JOSEPH
WARREN,
AND HIS ASSOCIATES,
WHO WERE SLAIN ON THIS
MEMORABLE SPOT,
June 17, 1775.

"None but those who set a just value upon the blessings of Liberty are worthy to enjoy her.
"In vain we toiled; in vain we fought; — we
bled in vain, if you, our offspring, want
valor to repel the assaults of her invaders."

***

When the present monument was completed, the Masonic Lodge placed a beautiful model of the old monument inside of the new one. This model stands directly in front of the entrance.

The conspicuous figure of Gen. Joseph Warren will always rise in the imagination whenever the American Revolution is mentioned, or the pages of its history are opened. Due and deserved honors have been paid to his memory, which will last when the firm granite column, which marks the spot given where he yielded up his life's blood in the cause of liberty, shall have given place to other memorials, perhaps in other less sacred causes.[2]

[1] The inscription "aged 35" is an error. Warren had turned 34 years old only 6 six days before being killed at Bunker Hill.
[2] From The History and Antiques of Boston, The Capital of Massachusetts and Metropolis of New England, From Its Settlement in 1630, to the Year 1770, also, Introductory History of the Discovery and Settlement of New England by Samuel Gardner Drake. The Masonic monument was eventually replaced by the Bunker Hill Monument and the golden urn is no longer on public display.

Engraving from Panoramic view from Bunker Hill Monument, Redding & Co. 1848.

Remembering Joseph Warren

On June 17, 1824, the Bunker Hill Monument Association published a letterpress broadside that proposed a monument be constructed in memory of the Battle of Bunker Hill. Contributing $5 to the cause earned donors a membership certificate. Upon acquiring a large field on Breed's Hill (where the battle had actually taken place), a design was agreed upon and construction begun. General Marquis de Lafayette was given the honor to lay the cornerstone on June 17, 1825. Lafayette, a wealthy French aristocrat at age 20, had traveled to America to serve under General George Washington. Lafayette became a Major General and battlefield hero. He was very influential in France's decision to align with America against the British, a decision that brought the war to a swift close. Washington, who had no biological sons, and Lafayette, who had lost his father at a young age, developed an adoptive father and son relationship. Years later Lafayette returned from

homeland France to America as the "Hero of Two Worlds" at the laying of the cornerstone of the Bunker Hill Monument. The grounds of Bunker Hill was a spectacle as Daniel Webster gave the oration. Speaking to Lafayette, Webster links the cause and memory to Joseph Warren, *"Sir, you have assisted us in laying the foundation of this structure. You have heard us rehearse, with our feeble commendation, the names of departed patriots. Monuments and eulogy belong to the dead. We give them this day to Warren and his associates."* Eighteen years after Lafayette had laid the cornerstone, in which time there were driblets of funding and intermittent construction, the Bunker Hill Monument Association celebrated the completion of the historic landmark on June 17, 1843.

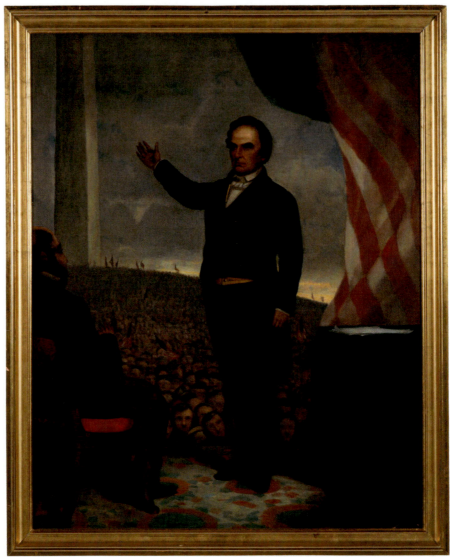

Imaged by Heritage Auctions, HA.com

An unsigned oil on canvas, measuring 29" X 36", depicting Daniel Webster delivering a speech at the ceremonies marking the completion of the Bunker Hill Monument on June 17, 1843. Webster had appeared there in the same capacity when the cornerstone was laid eighteen years prior. He stands on the speaker's platform gesturing towards the completed monument before a vast multitude of onlookers. The painting was unsigned and undated, but likely made contemporaneously with the event by a skilled folk artist.
Description and image courtesy of Heritage Auctions.

Remembering Joseph Warren

Let us remember Warren, and the brave men who laid down their lives for their country's honor and freedom. Let us hallow the battle-fields of the Revolution.

Reverend T. Whittemore, 1851

✱✱✱

"*It occurs to me, as a glorious reminiscence, that forty-nine years after General Warren fell, it was my privilege to be present when fourteen of the survivors of the battle, the anniversary of which you are to commemorate — all at that time residents of this town — were assembled under the hospitable roof*

WHERE WARREN FELL.—From a Sketch by E. La Moss.—[See Page 566.]

Take reverend steps upon this hallow ground, and look there at the tablet that reads, "Here Warren Fell, June 17, 1775"

of one of their number. They have passed away with the generation of the revolutionary epoch. There is no survivor now. Rejecting all sentiments and opinions calculated to lower our estimate of what the valor and wisdom of the fathers of the Republic achieved, let us manifest our reverence for their memory, not only by the erection of suitable monuments, but by taking the more earnest heed to their example and precepts"

Franklin Pierce, June 15, 1857.

***

"Joseph Warren was the intimate friend of my father [Josiah Quincy II], his family physician, inseparably united to each other by common feelings of indignation at the wrongs done and the sufferings inflicted on their country. These friends and correspondents were associated, in life and in death, by like feelings and spirit. In 1774, my father, then in full professional business and high standing at the bar, left his prospects and his family, at the earnest solicitation of Joseph Warren, Samuel Adams, and others of kindred patriotic zeal, and embarked for London for the

Major Gen. Joseph Warren, Slain at the Battle of Bunker Hill June 17, 1775. Engraved by J. Norman. Original in the John Carter Brown Library at Brown University.

purpose of confidentially communicating their wishes and views to the friends of America in England. His mission was carefully concealed from the public, lest the enemies of the American cause should devise means to counteract his influence. After fulfilling its object with an intensity of interest and assiduity to which his health became a victim, against the express will of his physician, at the request of Dr. Franklin and other friends of the colonies, he embarked for Boston, bearing with him confidential communications to the American patriots, which they dared not entrust to letters. The voyage terminated his existence.

On the 26th of April, 1775, when dying, within sight of his native shore, in the harbour of Cape Ann, he declared "Ae had but one desire, but one prayer, which was that he might live long enough to have an interview with Samuel Adams and Joseph Warren; that granted he would die contents. Thus departed the friend and compatriot of Joseph Warren; not as he did "on a field ever memorable and ever glorious, but in solitude; amidst suffering, without associate and without witness, yet breathing forth a dying wish for his country; desiring to live only to perform towards her, a last and signal service."

Josiah Quincy[1], July 22, 1857

1 Josiah Quincy (1772–1864), American president of Harvard University (1829–1845), U.S. representative (1805–1813), mayor of Boston (1823–1828), son of Josiah Quincy II

***

"Massachusetts contributed to the struggle for freedom her full share of patriotism and courage - — yet I confess that, to me, Warren has always appeared the most attractive and heroic character that she gave to the Revolution. In him, boundless faith and intrepidity, perfect rectitude, great abilities, enthusiasm, and fervent love of liberty, were so united and developed as to lift him above most of his eminent cotemporaries, and entitle him to a place in that particular galaxy composed of the selectest spirits of revolutionary times. No man saw more clearly the consequences of submission to the pretensions of the British crown ; no man saw more clearly the dangers involved in resistance ; and yet no man was more determined or effective in awakening and organizing the spirit that led to our emancipation. I persuade myself that, from the beginning, he looked far beyond the special issues that seemed to exhaust the questions of difference, and fixed his thoughts on absolute Independence. And although cut down in the morning of his glorious life, he did not live to see the united Colonies acknowledged among the independent powers of the world; it well becomes us gratefully to remember how much his life and death contributed to hasten that auspicious day. I am quite sure that the people of the South would no more admit that the fame of Warren belongs to Massachusetts alone, than they would claim the renown of Washington exclusively for the country South of the Potomac — and this is doubtless the feeling of Massachusetts. Whatever may

be in store for the future, the past at least is common property. Is there not good reason to hope that these treasures of the country shall never be divided — that the political and social brotherhood our fathers formed shall be perpetuated through all generations, and that the Constitution they bequeathed to us shall be revered and maintained as the only sure bond of union and progress"

John C. Breckinridge, Vice-President of the United States, May 22, 1857

***

"...for though this Union may be torn, if it must be, by some madness or other, and though the sun of our destiny as a nation may sat in gloom and a night of darkness, and though fratricidal blood may flow by the hand of folly and stain the hearths of our homes hereafter, I can never forget old Massachusetts — her Bunker Hill, her Warrens, her Adamses, her Hancock, her hail — her sister hail — once to Virginia — in "times which tried men's souls." No, never, never, never! May God revive our Revolutionary feeling!"

Henry A. Wise, Governor of Virginia, May 25, 1857. (Four years before the American Civil War)

***

(RIGHT) "INDEPENDENCE DECLARED 1776." Designed and published by Joseph A. Arnold from 1830 to 1840; Thomas Moore's Lithography, Boston. A memorial to the Declaration of Independence and the American Revolution. Above the title, in Latin, "E PLURIBUS UNUM", translated "out of many, one" referring to our many people, one nation. Below the title are bust portraits of the first eight Presidents, with Jackson and Van Buren joining hands, symbolizing the birth of the Democratic Party. Beneath them is a scroll with Andrew Jackson's famous toast, "THE UNION MUST BE PRESERVED." Centered and standing gallantly is General George Washington holding a scroll inscribed "WE DECLARE OURSELVES FREE AND INDEPENDENT." He faces thirteen soldiers each drawn differently with varying frocks, wigs, and boots, representing the original Colonies—now free and independent States. The soldiers are flanked by flags: the revolutionary banner "An Appeal to Heaven" of 1776 and the American Flag of 1824. In the distant background, the raging Battle of Bunker Hill gives tribute to our fallen heroes and the rising cause of American liberty. It has been fifty years since the War of Independence began and the Rise of the Boston Rebellion has yet a long road ahead. The whole scene is flanked by two columns, representing "New-England arising out of Old England." The columns are topped by statues of Liberty (left with shield down) and Hope (right with anchor set). On their foundational bases are portraits of two heroes: the young martyr General Warren (left) and the distinguished, now elder, General Lafayette (right). The checked floor represents the floor of King Solomon's Temple in Masonic ritual and the dichotomy of human existence: good and bad. The allegorical depiction is both patriotic and promising, then and now.

Remembering Joseph Warren 101

The Battle of Bunker's Hill, June 17, 1775. With inset panel "Surrender of Charlestown to General Clinton". Painted by J. Trumbull, Esq. Engraved by J. Rogers

"*...and that gallant man, whom you in honoring honor yourselves, — that gallant man, who was the most distinguished victim upon that distinguished field, — could he have returned from it... he might have said to Massachusetts "Tell it to your sons in Massachusetts, tell it to your sister colonies, and let it be handed down from generation to generation, that here upon Bunker Hill was laid the corner stone of American independence, and cemented with our blood"*[1]

Senator James Mason, in his speech given at the Inauguration of the Statue of General Warren on Bunker Hill, June 17, 1857.

1 Note: Senator Mason making use of the legendary Spartan call to arms at the Battle of Thermopylæ as what Warren "might have said to Massachusetts".

∗∗∗

"*Who would fail to feel an additional throb of patriotism in participating in doing honor to the memory of the gallant young hero who shed his blood in this great cause! The news of the conflict at Lexington, borne not as now upon the lightning's wing, slowly reached a party of hunters, seated around a cool and shady spring in the midst of a dense prime-val forest of Kentucky, and by a common patriotic impulse, the name of Lexington was given to the spot, where now stands that beautiful and flourishing city; and one of our most beautiful, fertile and wealthy counties, bears the honored name of Warren.*"

Charles S. Morehead, Governor of Kentucky, Frankfort, June 1, 1857

∗∗∗

A 19th century Connecticut bank note with a fine engraving of Doctor Joseph Warren. Connecticut was the only "Colony" that Warren traveled to outside of Massachusetts. In 1766, Warren investigated the fabled healing waters of a natural spring in Strafford, Ct. Printed by Toppau, Carpenter, Casilear & Co. for The City Bank of New Haven.

104 Remembering Joseph Warren

"Bunker Hill Monument"
The American Parlor Keepsake,
Published by J.M. Usher (Boston, 1854).

"Gen. Joseph Warren", with an honorary uniform of a Continental Army Major General, engraved expressly for Grahams Magazine.

Portrait of General Joseph Warren by John Singleton Copley, commissioned by John Adams. Warren was appointed the rank of Major General by the Provincial Congress on June 14, 1775. Without having yet received his commission in hand, Warren chose to dress and serve as a common soldier at Bunker Hill. Several posthumous depictions honor Warren embellished in a Continental Army uniform according to his rank as Major General. Copley, perhaps under direction of Adams, left the work partially "unfinished" as was Warren's legacy. Warren was the personal friend and physician of John and Abigail Adams. Image with permission of the National Park Service, Adams National Historical Park. The original is exhibited over the fireplace in the Long Room of the "Old House" in Braintree, Massachusetts.

"*I am pleased that the custom is becoming more general, as our country is increasing in wealth and prosperity, of erecting statues to our benefactors. I prefer these to mere architectural monuments, since they not only tend to improve the public taste for the fine arts, but also to produce a more indelible impression of the character of a distinguished individual by the association of ideas connected with his personal appearance.*"

Professor Joseph Henry, Smithsonian Institution, May 7, 1857.

***

"Your esteemed favor, inviting me to be present at the inauguration of the Statue of General Warren, on the 17th June, was duly received, and has remained thus long unacknowledged in the sincere hope that no impediment might arise in the way of its acceptance. A most unexpected bereavement has, however, occurred, which has plunged my family into the deepest affliction, and places it out of my power to become a witness of the august and patriotic ceremonies of the occasion referred to. I should otherwise have united most cordially with you in paying our devotions at the shrine of the first great martyr in the cause of civil liberty, and renewing our pledges in support of the principles of self-government, cemented and eternized as they were by the blood shed at Bunker Hill"

John Tyler, Former President of the United States, May 25, 1857.

Gleason's Pictorial Paper, Boston, Ma. Cover, Saturday, June 18, 1853 Vol. IV No 25.

Note: Tyler fathered more children than any other American president in history. His family was dear to him and he suffered great losses. Tyler's first wife, Letitia, died in 1842 and four of their eight children had died, one having just past prior to his sending this grieving letter of regret.

"Colonel Thomas Handasyd Perkins, who alone has the great honor of being the originator of the Statue of General Warren. On the day of the battle of Bunker Hill, he was in the eleventh year of his age, and though then a mere boy, he was old enough to be deeply impressed by the striking occurrences of that day, as they were related to him at the time, and especially by the heroic death of the first great martyr of the American Revolution. This Committee had several meetings for consultation, and were at last brought to the conclusion that the most appropriate Monument to General Warren would be a Statue of him of heroic size."

Committee of the Monument Association Bunker Hill Monument Association, June 17, 1857

***

Col. Perkins heartily adopted the recommendation of the Committee, and subscribed the generous sum he first named. The Committee was determined to give the order to some American sculptor for the execution of the Statue. Col. Perkins

Colonel Perkins

had, in one of his letters to the Committee, recommended to their consideration Mr. Henry Dexter, of Cambridgeport, as a Sculptor fully

Henry Dexter

competent to undertake the work.

Mr. Henry Dexter, who required two years in which to fulfil the commission. The Committee took occasion to make several visits to the studio of the Sculptor, in Cambridgeport, while he was modelling from his design. At the annual meeting, in 1856, they reported the work to be in a satisfactory state of progress and they were then instructed to use their exertions to have the Statue ready for delivery, so that it might be inaugurated on the ensuing anniversary, June 17, 1857.

Remembering Joseph Warren

Photo by Tom Brosnahan. Travel Info Exchange, Inc. InfoExchange.com

"The Statue is seven feet high, of the best Italian marble, and weighed in the block about seven tons. It is draped in the costume of the revolutionary period, — the model of the artist, as we have understood, being a veritable citizen's suit of Governor Hancock, which has come down to our generation. The attitude of the figure is highly dignified and imposing. The right hand rests upon a sword, the left being raised as in the act of giving emphasis to his utterance. The chest is thrown out, the head, which is uncovered, is elevated, and, upon the broad brow, and the firm, manly features of the face, thought and soul are unmistakably stamped. As we gaze on this noble figure, we imagine that we see the original at the moment when the imminent peril of his country engrossed his thought, and the great idea of the time thrilled his soul with its inspiration. There is a spirit in the marble; and the old days come vividly up as you stand in the grand ideal presence. You seem to see the gleam of the British bayonets; you hear the footsteps and the loud words of the hurrying and excited crowds in the streets. Thus we believe the scenes of those days will be brought up to thousands of minds when it shall be visited in its place upon the grounds with which the hero's name is forever associated. The splendid pedestal which now supports the Statue, — made of a block of Verd Antique, provided by the Roxbury Verd Antique Marble Company, from Roxbury, Vermont, and prepared and finished by A. Wentworth & Company, of Boston, from a design given by Mr. Dexter, — is the result of this liberal contribution. It rests upon a solid foundation of granite, laid deep in the ground, and cemented firmly together. There may it forever rest. Supporting this noble-work of art, itself a beautiful specimen of American production, both, in material and workmanship, and a permanent memorial of the patriotism of the generous donors."
Bunker Hill Monument Association, June 17, 1857

"I accept the proffered kindness, and shall esteem it a high privilege to witness the inauguration of a Statue to the memory of that patriotic soldier and statesman who was amongst the first of our Revolutionary Fathers to answer his country's call when her rights were invaded, and the first to offer up his life in their defense."

William A. Newell, Governor of New Jersey, June 1, 1857.

Joseph Warren as the father of the republic. Titled "BUNKER HILL", Engraved by J. Rogers.

"The Death of General Warren" from a 1953 press photograph of the upper right panel of a bronze door in the vestibule of the Massachusetts State House.

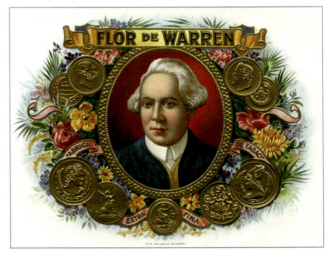

"Flor de Warren" cigar box label, Havana, Cuba.

Bust of Warren by T.D. Mulrey, 1859. On exhibit at the library of
The Bostonian Society library, Old State House, Boston.

"On the morning of the 17th June, 1775, eighty- two years ago, our Grand Master engaged in the conflict that has rendered this spot memorable. Regardless of personal danger, and anxious for his country's honor, he plunged into the thickest of the fight, and by his encouraging example, stimulated his countrymen to those deeds of valor, of which every American is justly proud. But it was not his privilege to survive the contest — he fell, one of the first martyrs in that struggle, the blessed fruits of which it is our happiness to enjoy. His death cast a deep gloom over the community; and by none was it more keenly lamented than by the Fraternity. To them he had been attached by ties, personal and official, for many years; they knew him intimately; they loved and honored him; and it was natural, therefore, that the sudden and violent termination of his life, should have been felt by them as an irreparable loss. The Masonic Fraternity have always been among the foremost in rendering honor to the memory of the brave and devoted men who sacrificed their lives on this field in the noble cause of American freedom".

John T. Heard, Most Worshipful Grand Master of the Grand Lodge of Massachusetts, at the Inauguration of the Statue of Joseph Warren on Bunker Hill, June 17, 1857.

✳✳✳

"...in its execution, has united the sympathetic ardor of the patriot with the conscientious zeal of the sculptor. He has adopted the original portrait of Warren, by Copley, as the basis of his likeness, and has no doubt attained as perfect a resemblance of the youthful hero, as it is now in the power of the art to produce. In his presence, and that of his work, it would be alike superfluous and indelicate to enlarge upon its merits. There it stands, let it speak for itself..."

Edward Everett, master orator of events, Inauguration of the Statue of General Warren on Bunker Hill, June 17, 1857

✳✳✳

General Warren Statue" Charlestown, Mass. Postcard by The Hugh C. Leighton Co. Manufacturers, Portland, ME. Circulated between 1907 and 1917.

Remembering Joseph Warren

"When we affirm that the men who on the 17th of June, 1775, stood shoulder to shoulder on Bunker Hill, and with unequal arms, and untrained as soldiers, but with firm resolves, resisted the assault of a well-appointed and disciplined army, led by chiefs of renown, were our own glorious fathers, and that what they did they did in no vulgar spirit of rapacious conquest, or in the impatient spirit of just and lawful rule, but as men, born to the inheritance of freedom, and when that was threatened, resolved to maintain it with their lives. We know that the gallant Warren, though commissioned as a Major General, rushed to the field as a volunteer, claiming no command, but seeking to share the common duty with the common danger and when we say of him, that he was the model of the true citizen soldier, we can appeal with confidence to admitted and well-established facts. He fell gloriously, on the field of battle, but he did not fall before he had seen enough to assure his generous spirit that the men for whom he died were not unworthy of him, and that the cause which he loved better than life could not fail"

Governor John A. King, New York, 1857

***

Life-sized bust and statue of Joseph Warren by Henry Dexter on display at Grand Lodge of Masons in Massachusetts. The building and library are open to the public at scheduled times. www.massfreemasonry.org

On July 4, 1910, the General Joseph Warren Chapter of the Daughters of the American Revolution (DAR), in Warren, Pennsylvania unveiled the statue of General Joseph Warren in the park, city, and county that had been named after him. The gallant statue made of bronze was made by renowned sculptor Richard Bock. The granite pedestal is ten and a half feet tall with bronze plates on each side. One plate honors the memory of General Warren while the others bear the names of the American war veterans who had lived in Warren County, Pa.

The Warren Bronze Monument in Roxbury created by Paul Wayland Bartlett (1865-1925), dedicated to the City of Roxbury in 1904. From 1904 to 1968, the monument and pedestal stood honorably on the street that bears his name in Roxbury. In 1968, the statue of Warren was removed by city officials to accommodate a road widening project. In 1969, the bronze figure, without its monument pedestal, was placed at the Roxbury Latin School where Warren was once a student. It remains there with some controversy about its ownership and limited public access.

Remembering Joseph Warren

Bust of Joseph Warren by artist Adrien Miller at his studio gallery in Seattle, Washington. After portrait by John Singleton Copley. Collection of Shane Newell. Photograph© Newell 2017

Original Ink Drawing of the Roxbury Joseph Warren statue by central New York artist Annette Gurdo, 2016. Collection of Shane Newell. Photograph© Newell 2017

Thanks to the diligent work of R.W. Stan Gaw, R.W. Glenn Kubick, and R.W. Robert Vartanian, The Joseph Warren Project began as a reverent and ambitious cause to place a statue of General Joseph Warren at his grave site at the Forrest Hills Cemetery. As the obstacles mounted, supporters rallied to complete the project. The bronze statue was created by Sculptor Robert Shure of Skylight Studios. Honorably dedicated on October 22, 2016 by the 6th Massachusetts Masonic District, Forrest Hills Cemetery and the Grand Lodge of Masons of Massachusetts in large ceremony of Masons, historians, authors, and Warren descendants. Photo: By Hoyom (Own work)
[CC BY-SA 4.0 (https://creativecommons.org/licenses/by-sa/4.0)], via Wikimedia Commons

Remembering Joseph Warren

The Joseph Warren Distinguished Service Medal was first created in 1930. It is one of the highest honors given by the Grand Lodge of Masons of Massachusetts, second only to the Henry Price Medal in Masonic honors. It is the highest honor any State Lodge can bestow upon a member that has faithfully and usefully served his Lodge and community. Extending from Freemasonry there are separate sub-fraternities that issue Joseph Warren Commandery medals and commemorative Triennial medals to its distinguished members. Many of the Triennial medals are embossed with the "Birth Place of Gen. Joseph Warren" on the front and the location of the State Lodge. The Commandery medals are often very colorful and ornate jewels that become family heirlooms and collectible treasures. Beyond fraternal honors, Warren County, New York and Warren, Maine, in 1913 and 1976 respectively, issued centennial medals in honor of their namesake with a relief bust of Joseph Warren on the medallion front. The silver 1913 Warren County Centennial Celebration Medal is exceedingly rare. The Bunker Hill Centennial Anniversary Medal, struck in silver and gold colors, issued in 1875. One side depicts the Bunker Hill Monument and the other side a relief sculpture of John Trumbull's iconic painting "The Death of General Warren at the Battle of Bunker Hill..

Remembering Joseph Warren

Scale reproduction of the original John Singleton Copley painting of Joseph Warren about 1765, by painter Bradley Stevens. License and permission from the Museum of Fine Art, Boston.
(Media License #16-35776-TL).
Collection of Shane Newell.
Photograph© Newell 2017

Bradley Stevens is one of America's leading realist painters. His paintings have been commissioned on a large scale for public and private spaces. He has reproduced historical portraits for the White House, U.S. Department of State, U.S. House of Representatives, U.S. Embassy in Paris, National Portrait Gallery, and Monticello. In January 2002, the Smithsonian Institution commissioned him to reproduce Gilbert Stuart's Lansdowne portrait of George Washington. The painting now hangs in Mount Vernon. In September 2006, Stevens completed an original historical mural commemorating the Connecticut Compromise of 1787 for the U.S. Senate. The mural is installed in the Senate Reception Room, adjacent to the Senate Chambers in the U.S. Capitol.

Eulogy at the King's Chapel in Boston

"HE was blessed with a Complacency of Disposition, and Equanimity of Temper, which peculiarly endeared him to his Friends; and which, added to the Deportment of the Gentleman, commanded Reverence and Esteem even from his Enemies.

SUCH was the tender Sensibility of his Soul, that he need but see Distress to feel it, and contribute to its Relief.—He was deaf to the Calls of Interest even in the Course of his Profession; and wherever he beheld an indigent Object, which claimed his healing Skill, he administered it, without even the Hope of any other Reward, than that which resulted from the Reflection of having so far promoted the Happiness of his Fellow Men.

When the Liberties of America were attacked, he appeared an early Champion in the Contest; and tho' his Knowledge and Abilities would have insured Riches and Preferment' yet he nobly withstood the fascinating Charm, tossed Fortune back her Plume, and pursued the inflexible Purpose of his Soul, in guiltless Competence.

... —and when thy Glory shall have faded like the Western Sunbeam—the Name and the Virtues of WARREN shall remain immortal."

Perez Morton, Excerpts from an Oration delivered at the King's Chapel in Boston, April 8, 1776

***

Epilogue

In 1775, the death of Joseph Warren had united the Colonies in a fight for liberty and freedom. In 1875, the life of Joseph Warren and the Bunker Hill Monument symbolized our united spirit to become one free nation. The Bunker Hill Centennial was one of the most celebrated events in our nation's early history. On June 17, 1875 the streets of Boston and Charlestown were filled with grand parades, Masonic ceremonies and patriotic speeches. It was the glorious reunion between States that had been separated by the Civil War only a decade earlier. In 2025, we will celebrate our country's Sestercentennial Anniversary. By remembering Joseph Warren and the principles of our indivisible nation, perhaps we shall welcome our 250th year with greater reverence and patriotism.

Shane A. Newell

Joseph Warren Bibliography

Stories about General Warren in Relation to the Fifth of March Massacre and the Battle of Bunker Hill.
A small and very rare book written by "A Lady of Boston." The "Lady" was subsequently revealed to be Rebecca Warren Brown, the daughter of Dr. John Warren and niece of Dr. Joseph Warren. As the first exclusive biography about Joseph Warren, it is a lovely tribute by an adoring niece. The book dialogs a bedtime story about the heroic General and his sacrifice for American liberty. Rebecca inherited the only portrait made of Joseph Warren during his lifetime, the John Singleton Copley portrait circa 1765. The painting was passed down to Rebecca's son, Buckminster Brown, and, in 1895, gifted to the Museum of Fine Arts, Boston where it resides today. Published by James Loring of Boston, 1835.

Spark's American Biography, Volume X.
From a series of biographies written by the energetic historian, Jared Sparks (1789-1866). Sparks published twenty-five volumes titled "The Library of American Biographies Conducted by Jared Sparks." The series contains sixty biographies, although Sparks wrote only eight of them. Volume X contains a concise and well-written section entitled "Life of Joseph Warren," written by Alexander H. Everett. As an American ambassador, Alexander was a well-respected man of letters in Boston and the brother of famed Bunker Hill orator, Edward Everett. Published by Hilliard, Gray & Co. London, Richard James Kennett, 1839.

The Life and Times of Joseph Warren
The first comprehensive Warren biography written by Boston's leading biographer for much of the nineteenth century, Richard Frothingham. The work contains unverified stories and accounts of Warren's young life and brave exploits. Nonetheless, the book stands as a work of importance and historical significance. Reading this hefty work is no small undertaking, but for those who enjoy turning pages of an old leather-bound book with toned crispy pages, finding an original volume is rewarding. Boston: Little, Brown, & Company, 1865.

Joseph Warren: Physician, Politician, Patriot
John Cary wrote the first "modern day" biography nearly a century after the Frothingham book. Cary

is the first biographer to consider it necessary to "restore" Warren's place in American history. The Preface points out that Warren's legacy was lost among the more romanticized characters that were, historically speaking, secondary compared to Warren. Cary's book is very well-written and introduces Warren to the twentieth-century reader. Published by University of Illinois Press, Urbana, 1961.

Liberty's Martyr: The Story of Dr. Joseph Warren.
A novelized tribute written by Janet Uhlar with fictional dialog between Warren and his family and comrades. Uhlar's work isn't intended to be a biography, but more of an introduction to Warren and his legacy. Published by Dog Ear Publishing, Indianapolis, IN, 2009.

With Fire and Sword: The Battle of Bunker Hill and the Beginning of the American Revolution
A compelling narrative history with Warren as the central character written by James L. Nelson. For me, this was the most enjoyable reading I've had about events between 1770 and 1775. Nelson is a diligent historian and gifted storyteller with loyal readers. A beautifully crafted account of the Boston Rebellion, I happily recommend reading this book. Thorndike Press, a part of Gale, Cengage Learning, 2011.

Dr. Joseph Warren, The Boston Tea Party, Bunker Hill and the Birth of American Liberty
An extensive biography by Dr. Samuel A. Forman. With medical and historical scholarship, Dr. Forman's work is well-written and nearly forensic in its details. Widely published, Forman's book may be the most accessible work to date and is surely helpful in restoring Warren's place in American history. Gretna, Pelican Publishing Company, 2012.

Bunker Hill: A City, A Siege, A Revolution
A masterpiece by the bestselling author and historian, Nathaniel Philbrick. I've read nearly every book written by Philbrick and each has occupied my mind with a time-traveling experience. Much broader than a biography, Philbrick gives a full history of the Boston Rebellion in his classic story style. Published by the Penguin Group: Penguin Books, New York, NY, 2013.

Founding Martyr: The Life and Death of Dr. Joseph Warren, the American Revolution's Lost Hero
Written by Christian Di Spigna, a well-respected historian, educator, and frequent speaker at Colonial Williamsburg. I was able to read a proof copy of this book before its scheduled release of August 2018 and found it to be a very enjoyable read. The deep diligence of Di Spigna's research has unearthed several new facts about Warren's life. Published in United States by Crown, an imprint of the Crown Publishing Group, a division of Penguin Random House LLC, New York.

Printed and bound by PG in the USA